Scaling Up
COMPENSATION

Scaling Up
COMPENSATION

5 Design Principles
for Turning Your Largest Expense
into a Strategic Advantage

Verne Harnish
Sebastian Ross

Published by ForbesBooks, Charleston, South Carolina.
Member of Advantage Media Group.

ForbesBooks is a registered trademark, and the ForbesBooks colophon is a trademark of Forbes Media, LLC.

Printed in the United States of America.

10 9 8 7 6 5 4 3 2 1

ISBN: 978-1-95588-418-1
LCCN: 2022902336

Cover and Layout design by Jun-Hi Lutterjohann.

This custom publication is intended to provide accurate information and the opinions of the author in regard to the subject matter covered. It is sold with the understanding that the publisher, Advantage|ForbesBooks, is not engaged in rendering legal, financial, or professional services of any kind. If legal advice or other expert assistance is required, the reader is advised to seek the services of a competent professional.

Advantage Media Group is proud to be a part of the Tree Neutral® program. Tree Neutral offsets the number of trees consumed in the production and printing of this book by taking proactive steps such as planting trees in direct proportion to the number of trees used to print books. To learn more about Tree Neutral, please visit **www.treeneutral.com**.

Since 1917, Forbes has remained steadfast in its mission to serve as the defining voice of entrepreneurial capitalism. ForbesBooks, launched in 2016 through a partnership with Advantage Media Group, furthers that aim by helping business and thought leaders bring their stories, passion, and knowledge to the forefront in custom books. Opinions expressed by ForbesBooks authors are their own. To be considered for publication, please visit **www.forbesbooks.com**.

The Table of Contents

Overview –
5 Principles for Effective Compensation Design

EXECUTIVE SUMMARY: *Compensation is one of your largest expenses and, therefore, one of your most important strategic decisions. It requires careful thought. There are many psychological considerations – and 5 design principles – in crafting a unique compensation plan that fits your culture and your strategy while avoiding drama. The goal is to get compensation right and out of sight; incentivize the right behaviors that drive results; and contribute to the overall energy of the organization – not drain it!*

"I gave a star performer a raise, and now everyone else is marching into my office, demanding one, too." "If anyone looked closely at our payroll, it would be hard to rationalize why we're paying certain people what we do." "I'm tired of losing our best people to the Googles of the world because we can't match their salaries." "It seems like our bonus plans have become entitlements – like we're just giving money away."

In my nearly 40 years of researching, teaching, and coaching in the scaleup world, I've heard many similar frustrations and concerns about compensation. To make matters worse, one Oxford dictionary definition of the term compensation is "something, typically money, awarded to someone as a recompense for loss, injury, or suffering (as in) 'seeking compensation for injuries suffered at work'." The irony of this definition isn't lost on us and explains why compensation is the only reason some people stay in a toxic workplace environment. It's also why terms like remuneration, pay, and wage are used in other parts of the world!

Most leaders wish they knew more about how to benefit from the strategic value that a sound compensation system can generate but can't find the information they need in one place. They suffer through all the drama that comes from bad (random!) compensation design without the benefits that should come from one of the largest expenses in their organization.

Listening to their concerns troubled me because I knew it didn't have to be this way. I had come across dozens of well-designed and effective compensation plans over the years and had identified some common patterns of what works and what doesn't.

I wasn't alone in noticing this knowledge gap, as I discovered during my regular Friday luncheons at Carlitos with my friend and co-author of this book Sebastian Ross. He had helped me write the three "People" chapters in my book, *Scaling Up*, and the topic of People came up often during our weekly gatherings over the eight years I lived in Barcelona.

Sebastian had been a very people-oriented entrepreneur, CEO, and investor for most of his professional life, and had recently taken a half-time stint as Chief People Officer (CPO) at TMC, a teleradiology provider headquartered in Barcelona, Spain, with 430 employees scattered around the globe. The other half of his time, Sebastian supported our writing efforts by researching, reading, and curating countless books and articles on topics like recruiting, organizational structure, coaching, leadership development, onboarding, and compensation.

Sebastian had known TMC and its founders since inception, had been consulting with the senior leadership team and was a good friend of CEO Alexander Boehmcker, whom he had recommended to TMC's board three years earlier. Yet he had never focused so intensely on the strategic aspects of HR (culture, employer brand, leadership, etc.) as he was doing now, helping navigate the People side of this rapidly growing business – a real-world crucible where he had already implemented several effective compensation plans and had the liberty to experiment further.

Both of us saw a significant lack of knowledge and attention to compensation among scaleups. And astonishingly, neither of us could identify a single practical book on compensation that we would recommend to our clients (or at least one that was less than 400 pages). The market was lacking a book we would want to read as leaders of our own firms, one that was curated down to a length mere mortals could digest.

We also felt that the topic needed to be approached from a general business vs. a functional perspective. For us, a People department is less of a group of functional experts focused on engagement and employee wellbeing and more of an operational unit that serves the business and supports its strategy. All People practices, including compensation, need to create tangible value for the company's stakeholders, especially for its customers. And approaching the compensation topic from this angle makes it more relevant and beneficial for any scaleup leader, not just the HR people.

With these reflections, we finished our meal at Carlitos Restaurant that afternoon – nothing better than a late Friday lunch with a good friend and a glass of Ribera del Duero – and committed to writing *Scaling Up Compensation*, the book you are holding in your hands (or looking at on a screen). What follows is a collection of stories, including TMC's, and proven practices, to help you design a compensation system that turns your largest expense into a strategic advantage.

Strategic Decision, Large Expense

How you compensate your people is one of the most important strategic decisions you will make. It can give you a significant advantage over the competition, support or hinder the culture of the business, and drive (or not) the behaviors you need to scale your organization. And since it is likely one of the largest expenses, if not the largest, fueling your business, it requires thoughtful consideration. Yet, like pricing, many of the compensation schemes we've seen are WAGs – wild-ankle-guesses – at best.

If this sounds familiar, this book offers guidance. We provide you with the vocabulary and the practical insights you need to design a compensation system that drives your strategy and minimizes drama while you scale the organization. We structure our thoughts in the form of 5 principles that will guide you in your design process. Each design principle constitutes a chapter in the book.

The remainder of this Overview is a comprehensive summary of the book. If you head up the People function, we recommend you read the entire book, and might even choose to skip this summary chapter. If you are the CEO or lead other functions or business units, we suggest you read this Overview and then dig deeper into the areas that apply to you. Here is a summary of the 5 design principles:

Principle #1 – Be Different: Aligning Compensation with Culture and Strategy

Lincoln Electric is not a place for everybody. The 125-year-old manufacturer of welding products, headquartered in Cleveland, Ohio, is a tough environment. The firm runs a merciless piece-rate regime that pays workers for output and quality, not for time. If you drill the wrong size holes or lay sick in bed, you don't get paid. In busy times, you might work 60 hours, when things are slow, only 30 hours (and you only get paid for 30).

What sounds like an exploitative sweatshop turns out to be one of the best-paying jobs in manufacturing in the world. A high producing assembly line worker can take home over $100,000 per year – $80,000 is the average. Approximately 60 percent of the amount represents an annual merit bonus, based on relative performance versus peers. The bonus has been paid out every year since 1934. (In fact, in the 1990s Lincoln borrowed more than $100 million to pay its people bonuses, even though it lost $84 million in a foreign-acquisition spree.)

Lincoln's compensation system is not better or worse than somebody else's. But it is different if not outright "strange" (as Dan Cable would call it – more on "strangeness" below), and that's how it should be. The first principle of compensation design is to *Be Different*. Strategy is about being perceived as different versus your competition. Ideally, all your People practices (recruiting, leadership, compensation) reinforce these differences. They must incentivize behaviors in your employees that your customers appreciate and make them reach for their wallets. Only then do your People practices create true value for the firm and reinforce your positioning in the marketplace.

Lincoln's comp plan does precisely that. It is strategic in the sense that it aligns customer expectations (flawless welding equipment) with the firm's strategy (positioning as a quality provider) and its culture (psychological ownership and attention to detail). And it is also strategic because it attracts people who can flourish in this culture and repels those who wouldn't.

Think of people's salary not as a cost but as an investment. This mindset is crucial if you want to run what MIT professor Zeynep Ton calls a *Good Jobs Strategy*. A Good Jobs Strategy means paying significantly higher salaries than your competitors, nevertheless, enjoying lower labor costs per unit and higher profits because your employees are more productive. Further, the investments in people foster behaviors that customers appreciate, differentiate your firm and put in motion a virtuous cycle where everybody wins: employees, customers and shareholders. We´ll provide several inspiring examples of companies who successfully execute such a Good Jobs Strategy.

When reading the stories of Lincoln Electric and many others that we share in this book, you might feel tempted to copy the compensation systems of these outstanding firms. But that would be a big mistake. Your system will only be effective if it is tailored to your unique context. Make compensation a critical part of your strategy, make it your own, and make it different. Chapter 1 provides inspiration and insight on how to do this for your organization.

Principle #2 – Fairness Not Sameness: Creating a Coherent and Flexible Pay Structure

"I feel that we generally pay people fairly, but very differently, and I don't always have good arguments to justify the differences in salaries and bonuses across the firm," noted Alexander Boehmcker in 2018 during a meeting of TMC's People Council (a sub-committee of the Senior Leadership in charge of the employee experience).

Is it equitable or fair to pay a 27 year-old software developer twice the money his 45-year-old colleague in Operations makes? Is it okay that a senior AI expert with no people responsibility makes more than a mid-level manager with a team of 30? Is it okay for the top sales rep to make more than her boss when the alternative is losing her to the competition? Should the C-Level executives who joined recently still receive a piece of equity?

For too long, this type of question had created noise and drama at TMC. With, at that point, over 350 employees, It was necessary to clean up the historic comp "mess" (in the beginning, we all have one) and implement a proper system. Compensation systems tend to develop organically with the growth of the organization. New elements get added over time as needs arise, but without much concern for internal coherence or structure. The result is often an incoherent piecemeal arrangement that is more a drain than a source of energy. At that point, scaleups need to go to the drawing board and design a compensation system that deserves the name.

The main goal of such a system is to create *Fairness, not Sameness* – the second design principle you want to keep in mind when going about this work. The key is to design a transparent and equitable system that allows for meaningful differences in pay between low, average, and top performers. Performance is not normally distributed, and thus pay shouldn't be either. Chapter 2 describes how to set base salaries and build a formal pay structure, with job categories/salary levels and pay bands, that create coherence but also accommodate for large differences in performance.

Fairness also means paying people a *living* and not only a *minimum* wage. Most leaders agree that inequality is a huge problem in the world. But few see that the way they design their compensation systems is at the root of that problem. In Chapter 2, we share several stories and ways to put this idea into practice.

Principle #3 – Easy on the Carrots: Using Incentives Effectively

"At Egon Zehnder International, we prefer to stick with the old-fashioned way to pay. In addition to base salaries, the firm gives partners equal shares of the profit and another set of profit shares that are adjusted only for length of tenure as partner," explains Egon P.S. Zehnder, the founder of the firm that bears his name, in an interview. "But we don´t pay any kind of performance bonuses or commissions. None," he adds.

Egon Zehnder International, founded in Zürich, Switzerland, in 1964, is one of the world's largest and most prestigious executive search firms. At most search firms, partners are paid according to the size of their billings. Zehnder is different. It doesn't even have a formal procedure for tracking the performance of its 63 offices.

The reason Zehnder sticks to this seemingly dated approach is to foster tight cooperation among the global network of over 500 consultants and the long-term view that it adopted as a core element of its strategy. Trusted, long-term relationships between client and consultant are key in the executive search business. Consultants who chase the next deal to inflate their bonus run counter to this approach. The compensation system also assures that clients can be freely referred to the office where they can best be served. Hoarding, common at other firms, is not an issue for Zehnder.

The example of Egon Zehnder illustrates how "strange" and thus strategic compensation can and should be. Zehnder decides to be deliberately old-fashioned. The firm could do what everybody else in the industry does and pay its people juicy commissions. Yet this would be unwise, given the firm's culture and strategy.

The main reason we share this story here though, is that it serves as a great illustration of our design principle no. 3 – *Easy on the Carrots*. Financial incentives influence employee behaviors in three ways. They help people decide if they want to work at your firm (*selection effect*), they tell employees what is important (*information effect*), and they can motivate people to try harder (*motivation effect*). Yet, in a complex and fast-changing world, it becomes increasingly difficult to design financial incentives that produce these effects and maintain them over time.

Chapter 3 lays out why variable pay is seldomly your best option to provoke a desired behavior. Most bonus plans fail to drive performance – instead, they become entitlements and cause undesired behaviors. We argue that individual financial incentives only work for simple, routine, measurable, and independent jobs and that your sales roles are likely the only candidates where such carrots will be effective. As such, we detail the characteristics of an effective comp plan for your sales team.

Principle #4 – Gamify Gains: Driving Critical Numbers Through P(l)ay

Breaking stuff gets you quickly in trouble at MiniMovers. Not with the client, but with your teammates. Because it reduces their paycheck. MiniMovers is a local door-to-door moving company based in Brisbane, Australia with 450 employees. Instead of paying expensive insurance policies to cover the risks of breakage, founder and managing director Mike O'Hagen decided to put aside 3 percent of sales for a bonus that gets divided up among the movers and distributed each quarter – if nothing is broken. If there is breakage, O'Hagen deducts the cost of breakage and uses the cash to reimburse its customers.

As a result, movers police themselves to make sure nothing gets broken. The amount distributed to each team member can be significant – over AUD 1,000. "And it doesn't cost anything extra, from the company's point of view. But I prefer paying the 3 percent, or whatever is left at the end of the quarter, to our people, and not an insurance company," says O'Hagen.

MiniMovers' breakage bonus is an example of so-called gain-sharing schemes. In gain-sharing plans, teams or even an entire company commit to moving the needle (often in a gamified manner) on a metric that points to a specific challenge of the business (productivity, spending, quality). This number is then tied to a bonus and paid out to employees when the goal is achieved. We call the underlying idea *Gamify Gains*, which is our fourth design principle.

The power of gain-sharing schemes lies in their information effect. By making goals specific and tangible, and tying a reward to them, gain-sharing plans inform people what is important. We find MiniMovers' plan particularly noteworthy because it is, again, strategic in the sense that it uses an incentive to convert customer expectations (intact belongings) into consistent employee behavior (handling belongings with care).

Chapter 4 leads you through a series of design choices for gain-sharing plans, discusses the effectiveness of such group incentives, and provides plenty of examples – some almost too good to be true.

Principle #5 – Sharing Is Caring: Getting Employees to Think Like Owners

Steve Rothschild, co-founder of Worchester, Massachusetts-based commercial lighting distributor Access Fixtures, wanted his people to think like owners and decided to pay them as such. For Rothschild, acting like an owner means, for example, watching gross margins and not revenue or thinking twice if a new hire will actually contribute to the bottom line.

To incentivize such behavior in his team, Rothschild implemented a profit-sharing plan where 20 percent of the firm's annual pre-tax profit is distributed on a pro-rata salary basis among his employees, representing 15 to 20 percent of their total compensation. This profit sharing is on top of what was already seen as competitive (fair) compensation. Rothschild is realistic about the effects of his comp plan: "My people don't work any harder because of the extra check they will receive sometime next year. But they take different decisions, which is good for the company and good for them," he says.

An even better way to instill ownership thinking, especially for fast-growing firms, is to let your people participate in the increasing value of the firm via so-called value-sharing schemes. While stock and stock options grants are standard practice among Silicon Valley-style tech companies, we find these tools underutilized in the vast majority of mid-market firms.

Profit- and value-sharing schemes are an expression of our fifth design principle *Sharing is Caring*. In addition to encouraging a sense of ownership, these plans are gestures of fairness and a way for owners to reward those who help generate profit and value in the first place. In Chapter 5, we provide detailed insights for designing both profit- and value-sharing schemes.

These 5 design principles, together with the many additional resources we share, provide you a framework for designing a powerful compensation system that drives your strategy and reduces drama. And as you delve into the details of each of these principles, take into account the following three additional insights when designing your comp plan:

Compensation is Not Logical, It's Psychological

Leaders don't do it enough, but when they do give compensation some thought – as with pricing (the other side of the same organizational coin) – they attempt logic and reason, pretending to have the "homo economicus" they learned about in business school in front of them. Yet, as Nobel Prize winners Daniel Kahneman and Richard Thaler, and also the later quoted Alfie Kohn, Daniel Pink, and Jeffrey Pfeffer have taught us, few human beings act fully rationally, and much less so when it comes to pay.

When money is at stake, people act more like a homo *psychologicus* than *economicus*. Unfortunately, this is why many compensation schemes have the oppositely intended effect – serving as a demotivator within the organization!

 TIP*: You pay salaries, bonuses, and other rewards in the hope of influencing behavior. As a reminder of how you do that, in Appendix A, we include a short summary of Dr. Robert Cialdini's (considered the "Godfather of Persuasion") six principles of influence applied to the context of compensation.*

Total Rewards

HR professionals coined the expression *total rewards* to refer to everything an employee values from their employment relationship. Definitions of the concept vary but generally include, in addition to compensation elements, relational rewards. These rewards comprise items such as a positive work environment, personal and professional development opportunities, and the company's reputation.

In this book, we focus on the monetary elements of your compensation system. However, when discussing monetary compensation, you always need to consider the total reward package as the different reward elements complement each other. Small and midsize companies have great opportunities to offset less competitive salaries and benefits with relational rewards.

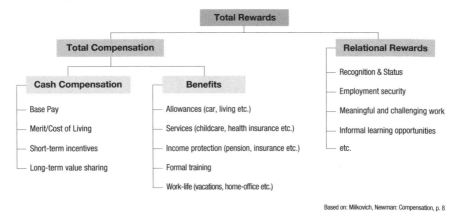

Based on: Milkovich, Newman: Compensation, p. 8

Total Rewards

Appendix B contains an example of how Nike graphically presents a total reward package for employees and candidates in an appealing way.

What's Not Addressed

There are two areas of compensation we leave for others to address – executive compensation and negotiating with unions.

Although all the principles mentioned above figure into setting executive compensation and should prove helpful in negotiating a final package, it is such a specialty field of compensation that we leave it to the lawyers and the 50 pages of fine print they create. Although the book is written from the employee´s perspective, Michael O'Malley's 260+ page book titled *Are You Paid What You're Worth?* provides some excellent advice for the design of executives' pay packages.

The other specialty area we leave for others to address is union pay. Mainly found in the trades and larger public companies, union negotiations require an expertise beyond our own pay grade!! Iconic leaders, like the late Herb Kelleher of Southwest Airlines fame, were grandmasters in maximizing the use of unions to further the goals of all stakeholders, including members of their various unions.

End Goal – Energy

As the two of us were writing this book, Sebastian asked a very important question "What is the end goal of compensation?" What we concluded is *energy*.

All of your people systems, including compensation, should be geared to increase the total energy of everyone in the organization. These systems should give people energy vs. drain it. So, to the extent someone's monetary compensation gives them energy or at least doesn't dampen their excitement for the work and company, you've succeeded.

Our intention is to help you create a compensation plan that drives positive energy throughout your organization. To achieve that, your plan needs to be clever and fair. Clever, in the sense that your

"Get pay right and out of sight"

systems account for the often-counterintuitive psychology of people and support your strategy, your culture, and your goals. Fair, in the sense that your people should feel valued and respected – so that they can forget about money and focus on doing great work.

The way people are treated at work has a far bigger influence on performance than the money you pay them. "Get pay right and out of sight" is a phrase worth keeping in mind when designing an effective compensation plan.

1

Be Different:
Aligning Compensation with Culture and Strategy

EXECUTIVE SUMMARY: *Being different is key to any effective strategy – and that includes designing a "strange" compensation plan that incentivizes the behaviors your customers and other stakeholders expect. But make sure your comp plan aligns with your culture/core values or risk it being rejected. This is why it is dangerous to just copy someone else's compensation plan. And don't look at people as a cost; they are an investment. This mindset is crucial as you design a compensation plan that supports what we call a Good Jobs Strategy. This allows you to scale with less people, who are paid more, yet with a lower total cost basis than your competition – a win, win, win in the marketplace.*

Lincoln Electric:
"The Best-Paying Sweatshop in the World"

Lincoln Electric, a 125-year-old manufacturer of welding products headquartered in Cleveland, Ohio, is not a place for everybody. Its culture is brutally demanding. Line workers compete fiercely with each other and only get paid for what they produce. Operators must even pay hundreds of dollars out of their own pockets if a faulty machine is delivered due to their mistake.

What sounds like a terrible sweatshop from the 19th century turns out to be one of the best-paying employers in manufacturing in the entire world. On average, Lincoln's assembly line workers take home $80,000 per year. Approximately 60 percent of that comes from an annual merit bonus, based exclusively on relative performance versus peers. The bonus has been paid out every year since 1934. But what's most astonishing is that all employees enjoy a life-long employment guarantee, after having been three years with the company. This policy has been in place since 1948 and has never been broken.

The merciless piece-rate regime with unpaid sick and vacation leaves attracts a few and repels many other people (25 percent of new starters quit during the first year). Others might reject the hefty penalty for faulty products as unfair and exploitative. But that's a good thing. Signaling to candidates who will be happy or unhappy in a workplace is a critical function of a compensation system.

"When strange people work in a strange system that feels like it was molded for them, it feels like coming home, and their loyalty to and identification with the organization skyrockets," writes Dan Cable in *Change to Strange*.

Meeting Stakeholder Expectations

Lincoln Electric is different in many ways, including its compensation system. And different it should be. The first principle of compensation design is to *Be Different*. Strategy is about being perceived as different versus your competition – different pricing, different delivery, different talent. Ideally, all your People practices (hiring, performance management, compensation) reinforce these differences.

The HR department (we prefer the People or Employee Experience function) doesn't exist just to make employees happy. Its goal is to serve the company's purpose and the needs of its stakeholders (a firm's chosen purpose is just a special stakeholder need). Every company has stakeholders whose support it needs to survive and prosper. None of these people are particularly altruistic; they all want things from you and get irritable if they don't get them. HR's ultimate job, as is everyone else's in the company, is to serve those needs – and as we mentioned earlier, to increase the combined energy within the organization.

Running HR strategically means creating a logical chain between stakeholder expectations and your HR practices, including compensation.

People Strategy: Connecting People practices to purpose and stakeholder expectations

As the diagram suggests, start with the end in mind and work backward. What do the various stakeholders (customers, employees, shareholders, and community) expect your firm to deliver? Next, how do you plan on delivering, in a differentiated way, on those expectations?

This "different way," which Harvard strategist Michael Porter calls *differentiating activities*, necessitates a certain culture. Your team must hold beliefs and values

> *"In large part, culture is a product of compensation."*
> – Alec Haverstick

that in turn reinforce a set of behaviors/actions which support these differentiating activities. The role of the compensation system is to incentivize behaviors in your employees that your customers appreciate and make them reach for their wallets. Only then do your HR policies create true value for the firm and make you stand out in the marketplace.

Change to Strange

Different strategies require different people. But don't expect your employees to be different if your People practices are the same as everyone else's. Everything you do in HR, including compensation, should reinforce these differences – the more extreme these differences, the better. Notes Daniel Cable, your People systems should be outright strange. This starts with hiring strange people but includes all other People practices from leadership to performance management to compensation.

> *"...start with hiring "strange" people"*

We might want to call Lincoln Electric's compensation plan strange. Nonetheless, it is a perfectly coherent element of the overall strategy and does what a reward system should do: It converts customer expectations into employee behavior. Stakeholder expectations (flawless machines), strategy (positioning as a quality provider), and culture (psychological ownership and attention to detail) are nicely aligned, and everybody wins.

Let's look at a few more examples of how the logical chain of stakeholder expectations, strategy, and culture shape the design of effective compensation systems.

1 Great Person = 3 Good People

One of The Container Store's Foundation Principles (their name for core values) is "1 Great Person = 3 Good People." The specialty retailer for storage and organization, founded in 1978 in Dallas by Kip Tindell and Garrett Boone, hires and trains people that are at least three times as productive as an average retail employee and then can afford to pay them up to twice as much as the industry average ($50,000 for a sales rep).

The firm doesn't look at compensation as an expense that needs to be kept low but as an investment in people and a key driver of the firm's overall strategy. According to Tindell, the approach was crucial to the enormous success of the firm over the past 40 years ("our compensation policy is one of the things we do best"). It helped the listed retailer grow to almost $900 million in revenue, 93 locations, and more than 5,000 employees.

The Container Store's approach to hiring and compensation is an integral part of the firm's meritocratic culture. It is as much a driver of the culture as it is a result of the culture. Tindell wants excellence and has the firm belief that performance differences among people are huge ("some people are just head and shoulders above the rest") and that outstanding people deserve to be lavishly rewarded. So, he carefully hires the very best, monitors and manages performance very closely, and then pays people according to their actual contribution. "I realize this approach contradicts the usual, superrational way of doing business, the number-crunching mindset that blindly tries to cut costs everywhere and assumes business is really about spreadsheets. [...] Most leaders are afraid of paying people well because they effectively don't believe in this formula," writes Tindell in his book *Uncontainable*.

Tindell's compensation system is a clear win-win-win. The employee wins because she's getting paid twice as much and gets to work alongside other great people. The company wins because it's getting three times the productivity at two times the payroll cost (why we refer to it as the 3:2 rule). And the customers win because they're getting great service from highly motivated employees. Everybody wins when compensation, culture, and strategy are connected.

Incentives are powerful shapers of culture. A good predictor of what your people will do is what they are incentivized to do. And that's why your compensation system needs to be aligned with your culture. Your design choices should reflect your fundamental beliefs about people and money. If you trust that your team will always work hard, you will pay them a high fixed salary. If you don't, you'll pay them variably. If you believe that competition among colleagues improves performance, you will pay individual bonuses. If you think cooperation produces better results, you will award team bonuses. Your comp system needs to reward the behaviors you consider desirable and penalize the ones you deem undesirable.

Generous Experts

TMC's growth story (30 percent compound annual growth for most of the past decade) was, to a substantial degree, also the result of its unique People practices. Since its inception in 2003, the company had positioned itself as a provider of sub-specialized, high-quality radiology reporting services for public hospitals across Europe, serviced partially during the European night out of Australia. TMC's central brand promise is to deliver the most accurate reports in the market. Keeping this promise in a field that develops rapidly requires a culture of "Generous Experts" – one of TMC's core values. Here are a few sentences from TMC's Culture Book that inform what the firm means by that expression:

- "Be thankful and keep your ego in check. When others proactively share what they know, we welcome this and don't take it as criticism, even if our own shortcomings are revealed in the process. Instead, we are grateful for the opportunity to learn and for the time that other people invest in sharing with us."

- "We exchange information freely and proactively to support each other's success. We are in this together and always ask ourselves who else could benefit from knowing what I know? We make an effort to document and store knowledge where it can be easily found by others."

- "The unique knowledge each of us generates from real-life experiences [...] is our biggest asset and most important differentiator. To leverage this knowledge, we must share it widely among ourselves."

- "We don't tolerate brilliant but arrogant team members. Their results may be great, but they ruin our culture and hurt the performance of those around them."

- "Innovation requires the free exchange of ideas across hierarchies and department borders. Everybody can have great ideas and must not hesitate to bring them forward. Our managers are approachable and listen to anybody's suggestions, independent of status, role, or tenure."

In summary, TMC doctors are highly qualified specialists who are nevertheless eager to improve their skills continuously, generously share knowledge, and are comfortable in a feedback-rich, egalitarian culture.

To foster these qualities in its doctors, TMC implemented a series of People practices that are quite unusual (not to say "strange") in Europe's healthcare industry. A few examples: TMC only accepts applications of doctors who are already sub- or super specialized (the vast majority of radiologists in public hospitals are generalists). Candidates for radiology positions must take a two-day, on-site assessment to test their reporting skills and knowledge, no matter how impressive their CVs are. Fifteen to 20 percent of doctors fail this assessment.

New recruits go through an intensive, week-long onboarding process at the company's headquarters in Barcelona. After that, for weeks and sometimes months, 100 percent of their reports are second-read by an experienced colleague until the doctor's reports have reached the company's quality standards. From then on, ten percent of all reports continue to be reviewed and, if necessary, corrected by another radiologist before they go out to the client (a process that allows precise quality management for each radiologist and is unique to TMC).

Last, but not least, the compensation system reinforces further the value of "generous expert." Radiologists' wages are highly equitable and fully transparent. Everybody is paid the same fee, based either on the number of reports generated or the number of shifts. There is a small adjustment for local purchasing power, but reputation, experience, tenure, status, not even the quality of reports influence a doctor's salary. "Diva" doctors, not uncommon in the medical profession, don't survive at TMC.

All these processes contribute significantly to finding and keeping TMC's radiologists humble and willing to learn. They foster behaviors that are of strategic value for TMC because they benefit the client and the patient. Humble doctors who learn and gain a rich experience on the job become better radiologists and write more accurate reports. More accurate reports, in turn, allow for better diagnosis by the referring clinician and better patient outcomes, which is what hospital clients and patients expect from TMC.

Core Values

Lincoln Electric, The Container Store, and TMC all illustrate how culture (and strategy) influence a company's choices about compensation and vice versa. Yet, to compensate people in line with your cultural values, you need a well-defined culture in the first place.

Do you have three to five core values that describe the basic behavioral norms everybody in your organization has to follow? Do you have additional specific codes of conduct regarding leadership, interactions with customers, ethics, quality assurance, security, etc.?

Atlassian's Core Values

For an excellent example of core values, search on the internet for "Atlassian core values." The suggested link will take you to a page that opens with a video. It features employees detailing how each core value is applied to everyday activities and decisions. Below the video is a list of Atlassian's five core values. Notice how each is titled with a phrase unique to the company (warning, some salty language); anchored by a visual symbol; and described in detail. You'll also notice in the lower right-hand corner of the page that Atlassian is recruiting based on these core values! However, like compensation, don't copy another firm's values – they are unique to your culture and requires a discovery exercise (read "The Core" chapter in *Scaling Up [Rockefeller Habits 2.0]*).

If you don't have your culture defined, your compensation system will incentivize some behaviors but not necessarily the ones you need to reinforce your strategy and meet your stakeholders' expectations. The logical chain depicted in the diagram on page 20 is broken, and your compensation practices will not generate much value and maybe even destroy it.

 WARNING: *That's why it is also very unwise to adopt another company's approach to compensation without a lot of thought. To the extent that the key to an effective strategy is to be different–different pricing, different delivery, different talent – it is the same with compensation. We've seen leaders attend an industry trade association or executive education keynote and hear a highly successful business leader talk about a unique compensation scheme – and then rush back and implement the same. You want it to be structured differently from the competition. DON'T just copy another company's compensation approach. Make it a critical part of your strategy, make it your own, and make it "strange."*

The Good Jobs Strategy

When executed well, as at The Container Store, compensating people extremely well can put a powerful flywheel in motion that leads to operational excellence, loyal customers, and increasing revenue and profits (which in turn allows you to pay top-level wages). MIT professor Zeynep Ton calls this virtuous circle the *Good Jobs Strategy*. In her book by the same name, she presents another four retail companies (Costco, Mercadona, QuickTrip, and Trader Joe's) who all use compensation as a strategic lever similar to The Container Store.

All four companies pay significantly higher salaries than their competitors. Nevertheless, they enjoy lower labor costs and higher profits because they use these investments in people to create a culture and behaviors that customers appreciate and that differentiate these firms in the market. Let's take a closer look at the case of Mercadona, a Spanish supermarket chain with 90,000 employees and 1,600 stores, founded in 1977 by a family of butchers from a town close to Valencia.

People Are Not a Cost; They Are an Investment

Mercadona's success story began in the 80s when co-founder and CEO Juan Roig implemented a counter-strategy to prevent the entry of large French competitors into the Spanish market. Roig's courageous approach consisted of lowering prices and increasing salaries to attract more customers and better talent. It took some years to get the flywheel going, but the higher salaries (double the Spanish minimum salary and 50 percent above the fashion retailer Zara) and a rigorous selection process eventually put the very best talent at the company's disposition. Once team members come on board, Mercadona invests $5,000 in training them in a four-week boot camp where they learn everything about "el jefe" (Spanish for "boss" and the company's term for the customer), store operations and Total Quality Management, an approach to organizational management based on customer satisfaction. They also receive intensive tutoring from experienced specialists. Employees are kept happy with regular salary increases (11 percent in each of the first four years), generous bonus payments of up to two monthly salaries, 30 vacation days, stable and family-friendly schedules, etc. All employees have indefinite contracts – there are no temps. "You need to spend money to have the best team. Just like you have to spend money to have the best location or the best lawyer," shares a regional sales manager of Mercadona.

As a result of these investments, highly talented, motivated, well-trained, and loyal people (the company only has 3-4 percent turnover!) go to work for Mercadona every day. They deliver far higher productivity (46 percent higher sales per employee than the average US supermarket) and are empowered to suggest and realize improvements continuously. These thousands of small improvements lead to operational excellence, which, in turn, delights customers, increases sales, and produces ever-rising profits at the end of this virtuous cycle. Mercadona set this flywheel in motion more than 40 years ago, and it is spinning ever faster. The company generated $25 billion in revenue and $623 million in profit in 2019. It is Spain's largest and most profitable supermarket chain and beats Walmart by a factor of 3x.

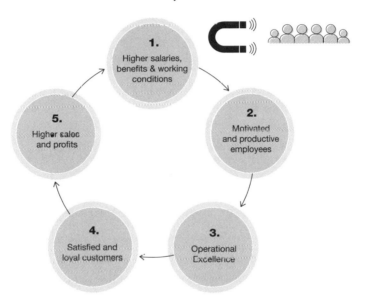

Flywheel of the Good Jobs strategy

Worry About What People Do, Not What They Cost

Again, the key to Mercadona's success is labor productivity. It has higher labor *rates* than the competition but lower labor *costs* relative to revenue. Competing on labor rates is much easier than putting in place a *Good Jobs Strategy*. But it is not sustainable and regularly pushes companies down a slippery slope to mediocrity or extinction. "Worry about what people do, not what they cost," writes Jeffrey Pfeffer in his classic *HBR* article *Six Dangerous Myths About Pay*.

Mercadona isn't alone in using this approach. Costco in the US applies the same philosophy. Its salaries are 30-40 percent higher than at Sam's Club (another bulk retailer with a membership model and Costco's biggest competitor); nevertheless, Costco is more profitable and grows faster. The Good Jobs Strategy is also not particular to the retail industry. It is rather a strategy pattern that can be replicated in many industries and firms of all sizes.

The most famous example is Henry Ford's decision to double his workers' wages, which Verne details in his book *The Greatest Business Decisions of All Time*. Goldman Sachs applies the same approach, paying its employees an average compensation package almost twice as big as the competition. Yet, it has fewer than half the employees on a per revenue basis and nearly three times the profit per employee.

The same for mid-market firm Maclean, a janitorial service company in Kuala Lumpur. Founder Simon Lim boosted wages for his janitors by 25 percent above local averages and then focused hard on driving productivity to the point that he has the lowest cost per square meter. Lim continues to win business and has no problem finding and keeping janitors. Or take Netflix, whose famous culture deck contains the phrase: "One outstanding employee gets more done and costs less than two adequate employees. We endeavor to have only outstanding employees." We could go on.

What Mercadona, Costco, Goldman Sachs, Maclean, Netflix, Lincoln Electric and The Container Store all have in common is that they hire fewer but far more productive people and then split the "productivity dividend" that these A-players generate equitably between the company (higher profits) and the employees (higher salaries and better work conditions). What distinguishes these firms is that they use compensation and other HR practices strategically. They, of course, care for their people and want them to flourish. But at the same time, they try to foster specific behaviors in them that make a difference for customers and allow these firms to be so successful in the marketplace. When there is alignment between what the market needs and HR provides, everybody wins.

To be clear: The higher worker productivity at these firms is not the result of higher salaries (as we will see, people generally don't work harder because they get paid more), but the consequence of getting the best talent on board and creating an environment where these people can thrive and be their very best.

A Good Jobs Strategy is not something you can quickly implement in any given quarter. It is based on a complex set of mutually reinforcing activities that need to be built out over the years. Compensation is just one element in this strategy, albeit a critical one.

Before we move on to more technical considerations of compensation in the next chapter, we want to share another, particularly impactful story to illustrate how choices around pay can drive culture/strategy and significantly alter the fate of a company.

A $70,000 Minimum-Wage

"You're ripping me off. I am not making enough money to lead a decent life," is what Jason Haley, a phone technician at Gravity Payments, told his CEO Dan Price during a smoking break in late 2011. Price was hurt, but the phrase triggered what became one of the world's most famous experiments in paying workers and made Price a celebrated warrior against income inequality.

Haley was making $35,000 at the time of the encounter. Gravity Payment, a Seattle-based credit card payment processor, had barely made it through the 2008 financial crisis, and Price had kept a tight lid on salaries since then. However, Haley's comment set off a transformation that culminated in Price announcing on April 13, 2014, that the minimum wage at his firm would be set at $70,000 and that he would partly fund this change by reducing his own salary from $1.1 million to $70,000. The move meant that just under one-third of his people saw their pay doubled, a little more than one-third got substantial raises, and one-third kept their salary because they were already making $70,000 or more.

A Media Tsunami

Gravity only had 120 employees at the time and struggled to make it even into the local news in Seattle. Yet, this announcement kicked off an unprecedented tsunami of media coverage worldwide. The next day, Price began receiving calls from ABC, NBC, CBS, CNN, Newscorp—and many other media outlets. A *New York Times* piece had been picked up by media across the world, and hundreds of thousands of visitors crashed the firm's website. The story created more than 500 million interactions on social media, and NBC's video coverage of the announcement became the most shared in network history. The firm was flooded with so much interest from the media, clients, candidates, and other companies who wanted to learn from it that it accidentally blew off the

US Secretary of Labor, Tom Perez, who called the company's main line to speak with Price.

We don't think the move was just a clever publicity stunt (if it was, Price is a genius). Price is the real deal. He has strong Christian values, a big heart, and

"...create a place where people could come to work and pretend they were volunteers"

simply couldn't stand that some of his people struggled to make ends meet while he didn't even know how to spend his money. "Philosophically, what I wanted to create at Gravity was a place where people could come to work and pretend they were volunteers," he said. "I had implemented our raise policy because I didn't want my people to have to worry about money, and I also didn't want money to be the only reason they came to work."

The Happiness Threshold

The $70,000 that Price settled on was not a random pick. Price had read a well-known research piece written by Nobel Prize laureate Daniel Kahneman and the British academic Angus Deaton. In their 2010 article, the two economists concluded: "More money does not necessarily buy more happiness, but less money is associated with emotional pain. Perhaps $75,000 is a threshold beyond which further increases in income no longer improve individuals' ability to do what matters most to their emotional wellbeing, such as spending time with people they like, avoiding pain and disease, and enjoying leisure." Price finally settled on $70,000 because he felt Gravity could not afford more at that time.

Despite his own salary cut, Price had hoped to fund the policy change with some additional business through the media coverage of the announcement: "I wondered if we could pay for a small percentage of the increased expenditure by generating awareness for the company. Maybe some businesses would hear about our values and how we operated and want to work with us," shares Price in his book *Worth It*. But nobody could have anticipated the incredible wave of positive reactions the move provoked, as well as some negative ones.

As you would guess, almost all employees were delighted with the decision, which changed their lives for the better in significant ways (though two senior people left because they perceived the raises for lower ranks as unfair). More than 10 percent of the team purchased a first home since the policy went into effect. Several moved closer to the office and reduced their commute. Many got rid of student loans, and, interestingly, several people started a family and had their first baby. More than forty babies have joined the Gravity family since the announcement.

Ripple Effects

We will never know what would have happened without the $70,000 policy, but it did not cripple the business as some observers predicted. Since 2014, when Gravity gradually started to implement the policy, the client base has grown by more than 75 percent, and revenue has increased from $15 million to $50 million. Profit also doubled, despite the added $2 million to payroll. Gravity did lose a few customers. Some felt the announcement put pressure on them to raise their own wages. Others feared Gravity would hike prices or cut back on service. Yet, Price made sure that neither of those things happened and was able to increase customer retention after the April 2014 announcement.

As if more proof was necessary, the Covid-19 crisis in 2020 has shown that the $70,000 policy is not only a generous gesture but a smart business decision that has made Gravity more popular with stakeholders and more anti-fragile. At the onset of the pandemic, the firm's revenues dropped dramatically because many of the 20,000 small businesses Gravity serves were severely hit. "We were losing $1.5 million a month and had three months before going out of business," Price shared in an interview. Layoffs seemed unavoidable. Yet, Price explained the situation openly to his team of now 200, and they offered a solution: Instead of layoffs, they suggested anonymous and voluntary pay cuts. This way, his team contributed nearly half a million dollars a month to stop the bleeding. Some offered their total pay; others anywhere between 5 and 50 percent. Moved by the generosity of his team, Price accepted the offer but capped all contributions at 50 percent. This gesture, together with other measures, extended Gravity's runway by six to 12 months, and Price is now confident that the worst is over and that he can soon pay back all his employees.

Further, as a result of the $70,000 rule, Price was also able to attract Tammy Kroll, then a senior VP at Yahoo!, as Gravity's new COO. Kroll took a massive pay cut to be part of that culture. "How am I supposed to feel comfortable with the fact that you're essentially volunteering your time in a for-profit organization? You're making what amounts to a seven-figure donation every year you work at Gravity," Price told Kroll during the negotiations. "Dan, it is worth it to be at Gravity. I'm willing to sacrifice the money," was Kroll's answer.

Another consequence of his sensational measure, one that Price had hoped for, was to create followers in the business community and reverse the quickly rising inequality in the United States and elsewhere. Gravity was flooded with stories from workers who suddenly got raises from transformed CEOs, in one case, even from an apparel factory in Vietnam where Price became friends with the leadership team. The fully remote software company Basecamp literally copied Gravity's policy and established a $70k minimum salary for its 84 employees. Coincidence or not, huge companies like Costco and Walmart also raised their minimum wages in the wake of the 2014 events. Ryan Buell of Harvard Business School, who began teaching a case study on Gravity, concluded that "an increase in the minimum wage is gaining momentum, both through public policy and through company-by-company decisions. One of the first snowballs that started this avalanche was Dan's announcement."

Gravity's story shows again how closely linked strategy, culture, and compensation are – and why in our first draft of the book we had many of the examples you'll read in the other chapters all stuffed into this one! Yes, strategy should drive comp, but sometimes, as in this case, it is the other way around. And culture is always in the middle. The $70,000 policy is as much the result of a caring culture as the culture is a consequence of the minimum wage. Think, for example, of Gravity's employees volunteering for a pay cut during COVID-19 or the brand-new Tesla the team bought for Price in 2016 from their own money to honor all the sacrifices he had made personally to make the $70,000 rule possible. Compensation = Strategy/Culture. So, please don't treat compensation as one of many banal HR policies. Comp decisions can ripple through your entire ecosystem and help you or hurt you.

Compensation Philosophy Statements

With clarity about how your compensation system can support your culture and your strategy, you have a good basis for defining your firm's compensation philosophy. A compensation philosophy is a written statement that outlines how people in your organization are paid and why. Its primary purpose is to serve as a "constitutional framework" for those responsible for shaping and operating the compensation system.

Many big companies have their *compensation philosophy* nailed and are well known for it in the market. PwC, for example, pays little but develops its people to land big jobs. Unilever offers great management training (among other things you learn its cookie-cutter approach to brand management) with almost guaranteed promotions every few years if goals are met. Strategy consultants and investment banks pay people lavishly at all levels but make them work like dogs until they move either *up or out*. Startups and scaleups can't offer great salaries but long-term wealth creation and dynamic work environments. Whatever position you choose, you need to articulate your philosophy to manage expectations and weed out people that are not a good fit for your organization.

The statement should be purposefully philosophical and express the idiosyncrasies of your organization. Describe your beliefs and values regarding compensation, but not operational policies or the concrete mechanics of specific instruments.

In Appendix C, you find further references on the topic and an example of a compensation philosophy statement for a fictitious company.

2

Fairness Not Sameness:
Creating a Coherent and Flexible Pay Structure

EXECUTIVE SUMMARY: *Getting the mix of fixed and variable compensation right is key. Just make sure each reinforces the behaviors/outcomes you seek. Base compensation is rarely motivational — and raises are short-lived in their impact — so this component of compensation is considered a hygiene factor. It is only noticed when people are not happy. And in setting base pay it is important at some point to establish clear pay grades as the company scales. The system needs to create Fairness, Not Sameness — our second design principle. Performance is not normally distributed, and thus pay shouldn't be either. Fairness also means paying the people at the lower end of the hierarchy a living and not a minimum wage.*

Telemedicine Clinic:
"Cleaning Up Our Comp Mess"

It was budget season again, and TMC's People Council came together to conduct its annual salary review. The People Council was a sub-committee of the senior leadership team, consisting of CEO, CFO, CPO, and Director of People & Values (P&V), and in charge of analyzing employee feedback and overseeing the implementation of new People practices. One of its tasks was reviewing the adequacy and fairness of TMC's compensation system once a year.

When starting the review of the compensation system in 2018, the People Council, once again, came to realize that the firm did not have much of a *system* actually. Yes, over the years, TMC had developed a quite elaborate scheme to pay its now more than 300 medical doctors fairly and attractively. But compensation for the 130-people-strong non-medical staff had evolved organically over the years without much structure. People had been hired in a decentralized manner with suggestions for compensation packages coming from the hiring department. Within a department, managers made sure that salaries were more or less coherent, but there was no way of comparing compensation across departments.

"I feel that we generally pay people fairly, but very differently, and I don't always have good arguments to justify the differences in salaries and bonuses across the firm. If someone would find our payroll in the paper bin and start asking questions, I would struggle to justify the differences in salaries across the firm," noted Alexander Boehmcker, TMC's CEO between 2009 and 2019.

Is it equitable or fair to pay a 27-year-old software developer twice the money his 45-year-old colleague in Operations makes? Is it okay that a senior AI expert with no people responsibility makes more than a mid-level manager with a team of 30? Does it make sense to pay quarterly bonuses to the Operations team based on case volumes when more than half of these cases are now assigned automatically by an algorithm? Is it okay for the top sales rep to make more than her boss when the alternative is losing her to the competition? Should the C-Level executives who joined recently still receive a piece of equity?

These types of questions had been creating noise and drama at TMC for some years. With over 350 employees already, it was time to clean up the historic comp "mess" (in the beginning, we all have one) and implement a system that deserves the name. Thus, Alexander asked P&V to study the matter and come back to the People Council with suggestions.

The goal was to design a uniform system of job levels across departments, assign the existing team members to the levels and then, in a third step, define the minimum and maximum salary bands for each of the categories that should be observed by all departments going forward.

Discontent with Disparities

A little bit of work had been done a few years prior, when Ida Anderman, then Global Head of Operations, and Sebastian started to create some structure, roles, and salaries in the Operations department. Operations at TMC receives digitalized radiology cases from hospitals in Northern Europe and distributes them to a qualified radiologist. The department had grown to about 35 people across three locations in 2014, and the need for formal structures had become apparent.

Employee surveys had indicated for some time the team's considerable discontent with low and disparate salaries, a lack of career opportunities, and leadership issues. In response, Anderman defined five career levels (entry, specialist, expert, team lead, manager), associated each level with a minimum tenure, required task proficiencies, established training needs, and assigned a salary grade to each level. The entry-level salary was also increased significantly. The new structure triggered several positive developments. The clearly defined career paths facilitated recruitment and reduced turnover. The formal training program improved job knowledge and productivity. Several team members rose through the ranks and today occupy team lead and even management positions.

The P&V team liked Operations' career path and compensation scheme, but it was apparent they could not be applied companywide. One reason was the need for separate career paths for managers with direct responsibility for people and individual contributors. In addition, the Operations' scheme didn't accommodate for more senior individual contributors. Several TMC departments employed highly experienced and well-paid experts who wanted to advance in their profession but had neither the intention nor the qualifications to manage people. They needed a separate career advancement and compensation plan.

At the time of this process, TMC already had more than 350 team members and, as we have seen, setting fair and motivating salaries for all these people was not an easy task. Compensation systems tend to develop organically with the growth of the organization. In the early days, companies live from hand to mouth and generally pay whatever they can afford without much consideration for structure or coherence. But with growth, new demands arise, and components get added to the system. This reactive approach is almost unavoidable in the early life of a firm. But it will eventually result in an incoherent piecemeal system that is more of an obstacle than a facilitator of growth. Thus, at some point, scaleups need to design a compensation system that can survive the next decade, be explained to people without blushing, and, most importantly, support your strategy.

We'll see in a moment how TMC has resolved its challenges. But let's first review a few basic concepts around base pay and how you should set it to energize and not demotivate your team.

The Three Drivers of Base Pay

Base pay is the fixed wage or salary an employee receives in exchange for the ongoing value he or she contributes. Compensation experts Zingheim and

Schuster in their book *Pay People Right!* distinguish three elements that should drive base pay levels:

1) **Competencies** – In most organizations, base pay rewards skills, knowledge, and experience the employee has acquired, kept up-to-date, and regularly applies to generate results. The acquisition of new competencies is often the trigger to move people to the next level in the base pay structure (more below). But be careful not to confuse years of experience with additional competencies. Ten years of experience can mean ten times the same experience and unchanged competencies.

2) **Sustained performance** – The most significant influencer of base pay should be the employee's consistent and sustained performance. Spikes in performance during specific periods should not influence base pay. Those are better rewarded via non-monetary recognitions and possibly variable pay components (if certain conditions are met; more on that below) as reductions of base salaries are fatal for morale and even illegal in some countries.

3) **Relative labor market value** – Base pay is further influenced by the relative value of an employee in the labor market. Where you set your baseline depends on the attractiveness of your total reward package, but, as we have seen, also your strategy, your culture and your financial possibilities. These factors will determine if you should lead, lag, or match the market in terms of compensation. Cisco, for example, sets base pay at the 65th percentile in every labor market and offers variable pay that brings total remuneration to the 75th percentile. In contrast, other companies like Google are much more interested in performance and value creation than the alleged market value of a job. (More on how to find market references in Appendix D).

Not Motivational; Merely Hygiene

Don't be mistaken: Base pay is not a motivational tool. People won't work harder because you increase their base pay (at least not continuously). However, paying people below what they consider fair is highly detrimental to motivation and performance.

External and *internal* fairness is the most important requirement of any compensation system. Fairness from an external perspective means that you don't want your accountant to find out that other accountants in comparable jobs and with comparable performance in other companies earn 50 percent more than she does. The *internal* reference for fairness is the colleague in the next cubicle, but also the supervisor and the direct reports. Their salaries must be perceived as equitable in relation to one's own.

Famous work psychologist Fredrick Herzberg concluded that pay (alongside other extrinsic elements like status, fringe benefits, vacations, etc.) is a mere *hygiene factor*. According to Herzberg, pay is an element that can cause significant demotivation, but it does little to motivate a person. Here is some data to show how psychological pay is and how easy it is to demotivate an employee with an "inadequate" salary.

To begin with, for many people, relative pay is more important than absolute pay. What do you think people answer when you ask them if they would rather earn $50,000 in a society where the median income is $30,000 or $100,000 in a society where the median income is $125,000, assuming that prices are the same in both settings? A whopping 46 percent of respondents prefer the lower salary in a recent study by the London School of Economics. Social envy is very present in the workplace as people take pay as a proxy for their self-worth.

Even the person you report to influences heavily if you perceive yourself as correctly paid or not. In the countless studies that assess people's reasons for leaving (or staying) with a company, monetary compensation turns out to be relevant but never the dominant factor. The quality of your superior has much more weight.

"Social envy is very present in the workplace as people take pay as a proxy for their self-worth. "

For example, in a 2006 survey by Gallup on why people quit their jobs, "pay and benefits" was the second most common answer, but only 22 percent of respondents mentioned it (recent data shows that in the wake of the "great resignation," the importance of compensation in the eyes of employees has increased, but this is likely to be a temporary phenomenon). Other reasons for quitting, like the lack of learning and development, poor fit with the job (not playing to your strengths), unclear expectations, and no line-of-sight (not seeing how your work aligns with the goals of the organization), together have much more weight than people's salary.

One thing all these items have in common is that they depend on whether your leaders do a good job or not. If they don't, then money may be the only lever you have to make people stick around. In other words, the perception of being paid fairly (or not) is less a question of the dollar amount on people's paycheck and more how they feel about their immediate boss.

"People would go from feeling grossly under-compensated to feeling like they were compensated fairly simply because we made a change in the leader," says Chris Moody, President of the talent service firm Aquent and partner with Brad Feld at the VC firm Foundry Group. Is this *logical*? Maybe. But it's definitely *psychological*.

Gallup, which surveys millions of employees every year, has also not found any consistent relation between pay and engagement. To the point that pay doesn't even appear on Gallup's famous 12 question engagement survey (Q12). "While an employee's response to each of the 12 Elements predicts how he will perform in the future, his answer to a pay question is so bundled up in psychological complexities that asking it usually causes more problems than it solves," says James Harter, Gallup's Chief Scientist in his book *12 Elements of Great Managing*. "Pay is a status-laden, envy-inspiring, politically charged monster."

These studies all demonstrate what we already warned you about in the Overview: Humans are not rational, and much less so when it comes to pay. If there is something we've learned from Nobel

> *"Pay is a status-laden, envy-inspiring, politically charged monster."*

Prize winners like Richard Thaler and Daniel Kahneman, it is that people are irrational. Objectively, small differences in pay can have a significant emotional impact. Receiving $1,000 less per year than the colleague next door can easily be perceived as a massive personal insult.

No compensation system will ever fully accommodate for the complex human psychology that drives the perception of our financial rewards. But a well-thought-out pay structure can go a long way to reduce anxiety, social envy, and all sorts of drama around comp.

Leaders and Makers

In the startup phase, companies typically set salaries individually for each position, based on what the candidate asks for or what the business can afford. However, this approach can backfire once people find out what their colleagues are making. With increasing size of the company, you must introduce objective criteria for setting salaries. This is best done with a so-called pay structure.

A pay structure defines standard salary levels for certain jobs or families of jobs. It is used to objectively determine the salary of new employees and assure fair compensation across the organization. A pay structure consists of a series of salary levels and pay bands, each band with a minimum, maximum, and midpoint rate, associated with it. Jobs with similar internal and external worth are grouped in one level.

To assign jobs to pay levels, you need to establish criteria. These criteria can be job-based or person-based. Traditionally, you assessed the value of abstract jobs (boxes on org charts), independent of the person currently filling the position. However, today's evaluation criteria are generally a mix of both job-based and person-based. Purely job-based criteria are becoming rare because, in fast-changing business environments, responsibilities change constantly. The job you evaluate today can be obsolete tomorrow.

Large companies, in creating a pay structure, often talk about the need for a *job analysis, job description* and *job evaluation*. This can keep entire departments

"The single biggest driver of compensation today is not the job title, but rather a specific candidate's own skills, achievements, and capabilities." – Tim Low

and hordes of consultants busy with creating and updating such structures. Much of this is overkill for smaller firms. Here, we only want to familiarize you with the correct language and provide a practical example. And at the end of the chapter, you will find references to resources that can help you with the practical implementation of these concepts.

But let's now come back to TMC and see what kind of pay structure Sebastian and his team designed. In a process that in HR speak is called *job analysis and job evaluation*, the team looked at all non-medical jobs, described the roles, and then assigned them to distinct levels. Quickly, it became clear that the analysis would need to focus more on the person than the job. Rapid growth was leading to frequent changes in roles, responsibilities, projects, and assignments, making it impossible to assess abstract jobs (i.e., boxes on the org chart), without looking at the job holder. The second thing that became evident was that the team had to create two separate pay structures and career paths for *Leaders* (people in formal leadership positions) and individual contributors, which TMC ended up calling *Makers*.

For the Leaders path, the team defined the five leadership levels (LL) based on the useful leadership categorization developed by Ram Charan in his *Leadership*

Pipeline framework (Charan's framework has more levels, but they did not apply to TMC, e.g., Business Group Leader):

LL1 – Coordinator (role: supporting others)

LL2 – Lead (role: leading others)

LL3 – Head/Manager (role: leading leaders)

LL4 – Director/Executive (role: functional or business leader)

LL5 – CEO (role: enterprise leader)

For the Makers path, TMC defined these seven levels, in this case inspired by work done at companies like Buffer, Medium and Fog Creek:

ML1 – Trainee

ML2 – Administrator

ML3 – Specialist

ML4 – Pro

ML5 – Ace

ML6 – Wizard

ML7 - Maestro

The next step consisted of identifying the criteria that define each level, i.e., what specific conditions someone needs to meet to be assigned to a level. After intense discussions, the team settled on the following five criteria and four values for each of them:

1. **Education**: Formal education required to perform the job, not the education someone has (1. High school, 2. Bachelor or similar, 3. Master, 4. Advanced degrees)

2. **Experience**: Years of experience in other positions needed to qualify for the job (1. 0-2 years, 2. 3-5 years, 3. 6-8 years, 4. 9-12 years)

3. **Training**: Time it takes in on-the-job training to become reasonably proficient (80 percent proficiency level). (1. 1-3 months, 2. 3-6 months, 3. 6-12 months, 4. > 12 months)

4. **Time Horizon of the Longest Task**: How far ahead the person regularly needs to plan to achieve the most important concrete results for which he or she is accountable. The longer the time, the more complex the role and the bigger its impact on overall business results. A CEO's most lengthy task could have a time horizon of 15-20 years. A first-line

employee (we like "first-line" better than "front-line" since there is too much military vocabulary in business already) might have a timespan of only a day or a week. (1. Daily to weekly, 2. Weekly to monthly, 3. Quarterly to annually, 4. Longer than one year).

5. **Scope of Work**: Describes the type of work and the way a person uses knowledge. It is also an expression of the "size" of a job.
   (1. *executional* – carries out concrete tasks like comparing, compiling, copying, etc., 2. *operational* – follows a process or methodology, 3. *tactical* – determines the best way to meet goals, or 4. *strategic* – establishes plans, objectives, policies.)

The TMC team then developed a point system that allowed the scoring of every position against the five criteria (each criterion was additionally weighted). The sum of the points then determined to which level a person or a position belongs (for example, 11-16 points = Administrator; 37-40 points = Maestro).

For the Leaders path, TMC also applied these five criteria but added a few others, like the *type of objectives* the leader has (for example, delivering a piece of work (=LL1) vs. long-term viability of the firm (=LL5)) and, again using Ram Charan's language, the *work values* that should be prevalent at a given level (e.g., getting results through own work vs. getting results through other managers).

At the end of this process, each of TMC's existing team members was mapped to either a Leader or a Maker level. And with that, the team had delivered what Alexander had asked for – the compensation levels for the myriad of jobs across the organization were now comparable.

The reality check was to see if the colleagues in each level are actually paid similar salaries. And yes, after some fine-tuning in the scoring and the weights of each criterion, a reasonably coherent pay structure, similar to the fictitious example shown in the chart below, emerged. Some incoherencies due to outlier salaries (referred to as "management debt" – explained below) remained, but the team was confident that these imperfections could be reduced over time and that they shouldn't impede the introduction of the new system.

The number of grades, their spreads (the difference between minimum and maximum), and the overlap between them vary significantly between organizations. For example, a company that likes frequent and formal promotions will have more grades and narrower spreads. The starting salary for entry-level positions should correspond to the minimum of a grade and thus leave room for future raises. Overlap between the categories is important to retain room for merit-based raises without having to change people to another pay grade.

43

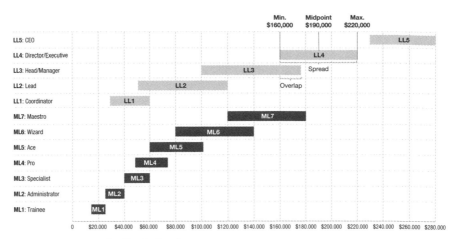

Fictitious Example of a Simple Pay Structure

In the fictitious scheme above, you could have a senior engineer at ML6, with neither the intention nor the qualification to become a department manager, who makes $135,000, while a colleague from a different department who has just been promoted to a manager position (LL3) only makes $110,000. There is nothing wrong with that. Top performers are vital to an organization's success and should be compensated accordingly. If you only tie pay to management responsibilities, you back yourself into a corner and only leave your people the option to compete for roles that don't suit them. Your employees need to have attractive career options without necessarily ascending to the top of the hierarchy.

As we have seen in the case of TMC's Operations department, you don't have to create a pay structure for the entire organization at once. The need for structure often arises first in departments that grow quickly and where many people do the same or similar jobs (sales, customer service, logistics, etc.). The number of tasks and responsibilities in such departments is often limited, and the activities are standardized. Entry-level employees learn them quickly and then look for ways to grow, increase their responsibility, and improve their salary. Inequalities in salaries and lack of defined career steps can produce frustration and turnover in such teams. Thus, the need for structure.

What you should avoid, though, is creating disparate structures in different areas of the company. Integrating them later into a company-wide system is painful. If you start with a single unit, build a flexible structure that can later evolve into a company-wide system.

Less Discretional, More Formulaic

Don't confuse structure with bureaucracy. Implementing a pay structure early in the life of your company can save you lots of headaches down the road. Once you have lost internal equity and people find out, it becomes difficult to bring the system back into balance. "Founders don't want to draw hard lines because they feel they need to do anything to get talented people in the door, but they'll end up paying for that decision later. [...] On the spectrum between formulaic and discretionary compensation, be as formulaic as you can," writes Molly Graham, co-responsible for introducing Facebook's first formal performance management and compensation system in 2008 when the company already had 450 employees.

All new hires and promotions should be tied to the established pay grades. There may be exceptions to the rule. But map out a transparent approval process for these cases and make sure it is followed every time. A common excuse for "special deals" outside the system is when a key employee threatens to leave, and management makes an outrageous counteroffer to keep the colleague on board. But what looks like the right thing to do at the moment will only create what venture capitalist and author Ben Horowitz calls *management debt*.

The following excerpt from Ben Horowitz's book *The Hard Thing About Hard Things* frames a term he calls management debt. We see many home-grown compensation plans, like other management systems, as piling on "compensation debt" which eventually must be addressed or can bankrupt the firm–literally!

MANAGEMENT DEBT

Thanks to Ward Cunningham, the computer programmer who designed the first wiki, the metaphor "technical debt" is now a well-understood concept. While you may be able to borrow time by writing quick and dirty code, you will eventually have to pay it back – with interest. Often this trade-off makes sense, but you will run into serious trouble if you fail to keep the trade-off in the front of your mind. There also exists a less under-stood parallel concept, which I will call management debt. Like technical debt, management debt is incurred when you make an expedient, short-term management decision with an expensive, long-term consequence. Like technical debt, the trade-off sometimes makes sense, but often does not. More important, if you incur the management debt without accounting for it, then you will eventually go management bankrupt...

OVERCOMPENSATING AN EMPLOYEE BECAUSE SHE GETS ANOTHER JOB OFFER

An excellent engineer decides to leave the company because she gets a better offer. For various reasons, you were undercompensating her, but the offer from the other company pays more than any engineer in your company and the engineer in question is not your best engineer. Still, she is working on a critical project and you cannot afford to lose her. So, you match the offer. You save the project, but you pile on the debt.

Here's how the payment will come due. You probably think that your counteroffer was confidential because you'd sworn her to secrecy. Let me explain why it was not. She has friends in the company. When she got the offer from the other company, she consulted with her friends. One of her best friends advised her to take the offer. When she decided to stay, she had to explain to him why she disregarded his advice or else lose personal credibility. So, she told him and swore him to secrecy. He agreed to honor the secret but was incensed that she had to threaten to quit to get a proper raise.

Furthermore, he was furious that you overcompensated her. So, he told the story to a few of his friends but kept her name confidential to preserve the secret. And now everyone in engineering knows that the best way to get a raise is to generate an offer from another company and then threaten to quit. It's going to take a while to pay off that debt.

Source: Horowitz, Ben. *The Hard Thing About Hard Things: Building a Business When There Are No Easy Answers* (p. 136). HarperCollins. Kindle Edition.

Performance Is Not Equally Distributed; Pay Shouldn't Be Either

A coherent pay structure does not mean you cannot reward outstanding performance. Structure should produce *Fairness, but not Sameness* – our second design principle. The key is to design a transparent and equitable system that allows for meaningful differences in pay between low, average, and top performers. Performance in most knowledge-based jobs is not normally distributed, and the difference in impact between two employees in the same job category can be huge.

Research shows that for unskilled and semi-skilled jobs, the productivity difference between the best and the worst performer can be up to 3x. For skilled jobs, the factor can go up to 15x and and even higher multiples when it comes to highly creative jobs like programming or design. So, you might want to ask yourself, how many of your average performers would you trade in for one of your absolute superstars? The number you come up with is most likely not correctly reflected in these people's salaries.

Typically, pay grades have spreads (remember, spread is the difference between the minimum and maximum salary in one pay grade) between 25 and 50 percent. That's not enough, especially if you have creative and knowledge-based workers with huge leverage on the overall success of the company (i.e., engineers, designers, product managers, researchers). Building broad pay grades (with spreads of 100 percent or more) and allowing significant overlap between grades are two ways of accommodating such outliers. A more extensive grade spread allows you, for example, to differentiate programmer salaries based on the technology a person commands (Java is more difficult than IITML). Overlap is also critical when you want to hire or retain key talent at a steep price tag, to the point that you end up paying the subordinate in the lower grade more than her manager in the higher grade.

Compensating "Stars"

Generously compensating "star" performers can pay off lavishly if your strategy is based on innovation, for example. Research by a team led by Fredrik Anderson from Cornell University observed a connection between innovative and successful software firms and the compensation schemes these firms offered to talented employees. Especially firms that operate in markets with huge potential gains from innovation (as in video gaming or tech firms) have a much greater return on hiring "stars" compared to other firms that operate in more stable markets. The study is another piece of evidence for our thesis that People practices, when intelligently linked to the firm's strategy, can generate enormous value.

Beyond any consideration of fairness or equity, for many people, pay is also just a way to keep score in the "great game of business." Thus, pay grades that max out too early at a mediocre "score" are no fun for highly talented players.

In any case, make sure that you make these design decisions with your culture and strategy in mind. If competition and ambition are important values in your firm, a large spread might make sense. If you want to foster values like solidarity and generosity instead, then you might want to limit the salary spread and pay people more equally.

 Key Resources:

- *For help with defining your own pay structures, we again refer you to the book* Are You Paid What You're Worth? *by Michael O'Malley. The book is written for employees, not HR professionals. Nonetheless, it is one of the better how-to guides on pay grades and compensation systems in general.*

- *Another valuable source to understand the "size" of leadership roles and appropriate categories is the book* The Leadership Pipeline *by Ram Charan, Stephen Drotter, and James Noel. This highly insightful book describes how the nature and the demands of leadership roles drastically change when leaders move through six passages from "leading yourself" to "leading the enterprise" during their careers.*

- *The hyper-transparent software company Buffer, an 85-person startup (more from them later), has shared its "Buffer Career Framework" which can serve as a useful reference as well. Among other things, Sebastian at TMC borrowed the "Makers" term from Buffer.*

- *If you need to create structure and a career path specifically for engineers, check out the well-conceived "Engineering Growth Framework" that the blogging company Medium shared in 2017. Another excellent resource is Joel Spolsky's (Joel on Software) "dissertation" on how engineers at his company Fog Creek get paid and progress in their careers. Beyond this, the software training and consulting firm Construx offers a 32-page "Career Progression Guide" for a variety of tech profiles, from product owner to agile coach.*

- *An additional resource is the* WorldatWork Handbook of Compensation Benefits & Total Rewards. *This comprehensive guide to all compensation-related topics offers in Chapter 11 detailed instructions on how to build a pay structure. Chapter 8 of the book* Compensation *by Milkovich and Newman provides additional nuances.*

Pay Review

Base salaries should be reviewed once a year for everybody, ideally synchronized with the budgeting period. Avoid anniversary-based salary reviews during the year. You have a business to scale and cannot continuously discuss salaries. At TMC, salaries were planned during the budget process in November/December, but raises were then implemented only in the February payroll. This gives time to communicate and negotiate new salaries during January instead of squeezing these conversations into the short and hectic month of December when sometimes the budget is not even finalized. And don't mix performance and compensation reviews. The topics are related but learning from performance feedback is difficult when money is on the table.

"...learning from performance feedback is difficult when money is on the table."

Valid reasons for an increase in base salaries are:

- Increase in cost of living
- Increased responsibility or formal promotions
- Merit-based increase for sustained higher performance
- Adaption of conditions for a certain role or job family to market rates to remain competitive

By the way: Although the practice is very common, tenure alone is not a good reason to give people a raise. The mere fact that people have been around for many years does not necessarily mean that they have become more valuable for the firm – sometimes it's the opposite.

How you determine merit-based increases depends heavily on your performance management process, if you have one. Larger companies have sophisticated policies, processes, and even use specialized software to calculate scenarios and manage raises. (Read Chapter 14 of the *WorldatWork Handbook of Compensation* for more details.) For mid-market firms, Verne's one-page planning tools (see Chapter 9 in *Scaling Up*) with individual and collective accountabilities expressed in KPIs, Quarterly Priorities, Critical Numbers, etc., are great ways to assess high performance that can then be rewarded with raises in base pay or the payout of incentives.

For smaller companies, a pragmatic way of reviewing performance and linking it to compensation decisions is for the direct manager to suggest increases and then discuss and approve them in a "compensation committee." CEO, CFO, and CPO should be permanent members. Invite department and business unit leaders to defend and discuss the salaries they propose for their people. Consider complementing the committee with one or two trusted, first-line employees. The view on compensation from the bottom of the pyramid can be quite different. And in the end, it is they who decide if your salaries are fair or not.

And remember, fairness and competitiveness are the only reasons to do this exercise. A significant increase in base salary might have a small motivational effect, but it is fleeting as people rapidly adapt to the higher income level and make it the new baseline of expectation. So, don't hand out raises to make people work harder. You'll be disappointed. "A raise is only a raise for 30 days. After that, it's just somebody's salary," says David Russo, former VP of HR at the SAS Institute.

"A raise is only a raise for 30 days."

Living-Wage, Not Minimum-Wage

Heath Ceramics, a home goods manufacturer with 160 employees based in Sausalito, California, stumbled over a very relevant fairness issue during the racial and social justice debate that shook the US in the summer of 2020. Heath Ceramic's owner and managing director Robin Petravic and his team saw that the company's 401(k) matching program (a US employer-sponsored retirement plan that allows employees to dedicate a percentage of their pre-tax salary to a retirement account) was only benefiting the higher earners.

"For years we've been proud of offering the same level of benefits to all our employees, but when we dug into the details of the 401(k) plan, we found that it did not provide equity for those on the lower end of the pay scale," he says. "Our matching program, through which we make employer contributions to match employee contributions, presents a particular problem because if you are on the lower end of the pay scale and can't afford to put your money into a 401(k) account, you get nothing, whereas if you are a higher earner who can afford to contribute a lot of your pay into your account, you get free money from the company. It turns out it's a benefit that builds disparity on top of existing economic disparity. If you're looking to create equity, it's not right."

To correct the perceived injustice, the firm did two things: First, it halved the budget for the 401(k) matching program and replaced the proportional payments with equal contributions for everyone, based on tenure and regardless of base salary levels. Second, taking the other half of what formerly went toward the 401(k) plan, Petravic funded a minimum wage increase from $16 to $20 an hour, from which 28 percent of Heath's employees benefited.

At first, not everybody was happy about this decision, but Petravic feels he did the right thing. Just like Dan Price at Gravity Payments, he did something tangible and meaningful to reduce income inequality and give people a living wage (defined as one that covers the basic needs of an employee and sometimes his or her family, including food, housing, healthcare, education, and transportation, as well as some discretionary income). And he strengthened the firm's culture: "Company-wide, enthusiasm was strong. We heard incredibly thoughtful comments, many from those we don't hear from often. From start to finish, this change was truly a unifying experience. We're so grateful to work with incredible people who recognized the importance of this initiative for the collective good," wrote Petravic and his wife Cathy Bailey in their 2021 New Year's Letter to Customers, Fans, Friends, and Family.

KEY RESOURCE: *Check MIT's Living Wage Calculator to learn what your people would need to make to have a living wage (Data for the US only). And read Amii Barnard-Bahn's HBR article (*How to Identify — and Fix — Pay Inequality at Your Company*) to learn how to run a* Pay-Equity-Audit *in which you compare the pay of employees doing "like for like" work and investigate the causes of any pay differences that cannot be justified.*

Shareholder value out of the pockets of workers

American companies, at least the public ones, stopped caring for their employees a long time ago. Of the $34 trillion in shareholder wealth created over the past three decades by US corporations, almost half has come out of the pockets of workers. According to research by Daniel Greenwald at MIT, 43 percent of the increase in share prices in the years 1989 and 2017 is the result of labor cost reduction, in other words, a reallocation of rents from employees (salaries) to shareholders (profits). In comparison, from 1952 to 1988, less than half as much wealth was created, but economic growth accounted for all of it.

Most leaders agree that inequality is a big problem in the world. But few see that the way they design their compensation systems is at the root of that issue. It's a sad fact that the majority of workers are financially weak, vulnerable, and living on the edge of disaster. That's true for the United States, but not much different for the rest of the world. Raj Sisodia, in his book *The Healing Organization*, offers some revealing data for the US:

- About 95 million Americans – 70 percent of full-time employees – live paycheck to paycheck.
- Fifty percent have less than $400 in the bank and would not be able to raise $2,000 within thirty days in the event of an emergency.
- Sixty percent are technically insolvent, which means that their liabilities exceed their assets. Most are going further into debt every year.

Small income reductions due to reduced hours, illness, or unexpected expenses and hourly employees quickly find themselves in danger of losing housing, utilities, transportation, etc. Who do they go to for help? Out of desperation and lack of options, people turn to intermediaries who provide short-term relief, but usurious interest rates, late fees, and penalties quickly drive people into existential financial troubles. And this is not only a problem for the employee but also the employer. Distressed and anxious workers don't perform as well, are absent, or leave their job altogether. And to be clear, these troubles exist, in part at least, because technically, until pay day, firms borrow money from their poorest employees.

The most sustainable way to avoid this suffering is a Good Jobs Strategy where firms pay highly productive people far above legal minimum wages and allow them to live comfortably. While implementing a Good Jobs Strategy can take years, measures like those at Heath Ceramics can be implemented next month. Here are a few more ideas to make life easier for the people at the bottom of your compensation pyramid.

Mind the Gap

In most Western countries, inflation had less impact on compensation in recent decades. But even small increases in prices over several years compound and reduce real wages noticeably. TMC had the policy, in some locations even a legal obligation, to compensate employees for the loss of purchasing power due to inflation during the annual salary review process. To give lower-income groups a break (and not increase monthly paychecks by ridiculously small amounts), Alexander (TMC's CEO) suggested defining the raise either as an absolute amount (e.g., $100/mo.) or a relative increment (2 percent), whatever amount was larger. The amounts were not life-changing for people, but they contributed toward living wages and kept TMC's salary gap in check.

With identical intentions but working the other end of the spectrum, some companies limit the gap between the highest-paid person and the median employee. Peter Drucker, the godfather of modern management, believed that a healthy CEO-to-worker pay ratio was around 25-to-1. Whole Foods Market had a cap at 20x, until Amazon bought the company. According to data compiled by Bloomberg, the typical CEO among the 1,000 biggest publicly-traded firms in the US receives 144 times the salary of his median employee. For TMC, the ratio has always been below 10.

Paying Frequently

Wholesome International, a multi-concept restaurant development company that owns 25 Five Guys and 6 Choolaah (Indian fast-casual food) outlets on the US East Coast, pays its team members weekly, even its salaried employees. Running payroll weekly or at least bi-weekly is something that European companies should consider, given that monthly payrolls are the widespread norm in that region. By the way, offering pay advances doesn't do the trick. Asking for an advance is humiliating, and the process is often an administrative nightmare for both sides.

Earned Wage Access (EWA) is another way of tackling the issues. EWA, a term coined by PayActiv, a fintech company founded in 2011 in San Jose, California, is a service that allows employees to draw on-demand a portion of their wages for the hours they have already worked but not yet been paid for by their employer. Employees can use their phones to transfer the money they need into their bank account or credit card at any time and as frequently as they want. Walmart hired the company to give their 1,4 million employees this flexibility.

Two Mints per Person

Dr. Robert Cialdini, the famous behavioral psychologist we quoted at the beginning of the book, shares an astonishing study that demonstrates again how *psychological* compensation is – and, in this case, how you can apply the principle of reciprocity to help your service employees increase their pay.

Imagine you just had a delicious meal at a fine restaurant, and your waiter approaches to present you with the bill. A way for the server to increase his tip is to provide you with one mint per diner. If he does that, his tip will increase by 3.3 percent compared to the norm. If he gives two mints per person, his tip will increase on average by 14 percent vs. the norm. Not bad!

But wait! Your server can increase his gratuity even further by doing the following: He approaches your table with the bill, leaves one mint in front of every diner, thanks everyone for their business, and then turns around to leave. Yet, just a few steps away from the table, he turns around, approaches the table again, and says: "I have to say, you've been such wonderful guests tonight. One mint is simply not enough!"

He then places one additional mint in front of each guest and again thanks everyone for dining at the restaurant. What do you think just happened to his tip? It climbed by 23 percent vs. the norm!

Teaching Financial Literacy

When designing people's compensation, you might also want to consider educating them on how to use the money they make. Many people lack basic financial literacy and neither spend nor invest their money in the best way. Raghav Kheria, Director of Kolkata, India-based Farinni Leather, a leather manufacturer and exporter to Europe for brands such as Massimo Dutti, Ted Baker, and Armani, spotted that need among his team of 250 and started doing something about it. In 2019, he piloted classes to educate his people on managing their personal finances, such as how to approach bank loans, credit cards, and stock market investing. He plans to roll them out to all his employees.

Joe McKinney, managing director of McVantage Packaging, provided similar money-management training for his employees. For instance, he discovered many were paying weekly rent, a much more expensive option than monthly rent. Others were purchasing many of their food staples at convenience stores vs. the more affordable grocery stores. Helping his employees get more for the wages he was paying them was as helpful as a pay raise, if not more so.

Better Choices

Providing people with a *living* – and not a *minimum* – wage, as Robin Petravic at Heath Ceramics or Dan Price at Gravity did, has some interesting ripple effects. Price surveyed his team in 2019 (five years after the increase to $70k) to gather input for an article in the *New York Times* and learned that a higher salary gave people the freedom to make better choices without having to sacrifice other aspects of their lives: "Parents don't have to choose between paying for childcare or leaving the workforce to stay at home with their kids. They don't have to give up memory-making family vacations in order to move to a better school district. They don't have to forgo their own hobbies in order to enroll their kids in music or sports lessons. They don't have to put off saving for retirement in order to save for their kids' educations. Younger workers don't have to live in an unsafe neighborhood or shoddy apartment in order to pay off their student loans. They don't have to skip doctor appointments because they need to pay for car repairs. They don't have to work a second full-time job at McDonald's, in order to afford to live."

Salary Transparency – Your Payroll on the Frontpage ...?

Most employees want to have transparency about *who* gets paid *when* for *what*. This has always been the case, but somehow baby boomers and Generation Xers never dared to ask. Self-confident millennials are different. They make sure that they get a fair deal. Sites like Glassdoor and CareerBliss make it easy for them to find out where they stand. Companies need to respond to that. And they do.

A growing number of businesses and public administrations are now very open about their pay systems, and some even make all individual salaries public. Buffer, the software start up introduced earlier, for example, is one of the forerunners of this transparency trend. The firm publishes every employee's salary on the company's blog and has even developed a mathematical formula to calculate a person's pay.

Whole Foods Market is arguably the largest company (91,000 employees) in the world that has taken this step. Co-founder John Mackey introduced the policy in 1986. The original goal was to help employees understand why some people were paid more than others. "I'm challenged on salaries all the time," explains Mackey. "'How come you are paying this regional president this much, and I'm only making this much?' I have to say, 'because that person is more valuable. If you accomplish what this person has accomplished, I'll pay you that, too.'"

But don't just try this at home. This practice is a recipe for disaster if you are not prepared. How people react to knowing their boss's or peer's salary is not always intuitive (remember, pay is psychological, not logical). For example, research by Zoë Cullen and Ricardo Perez-Truglia found that employees work harder when they learn that their managers make more than they thought. In contrast, people work less hard when they find out that their peers make more. Total salary transparency requires a very coherent compensation system and a strict application of it. Keep your salaries confidential until you have that.

A good way to test your readiness against these criteria is to imagine that your entire payroll is published on the front page of your local newspaper. Could you provide a rational and coherent explanation, ideally supported with market and performance data, for the difference in salary between any two of your team members?

For a rigorous analysis of the pros and cons of pay transparency and finding the level of transparency adequate for your firm, read the interview with

Bethanye McKinney Blount on the First Round blog ("Opening Up About Comp Isn't Easy – Here's How to Get More Transparent"). McKinney Blount has 20 years of experience in the field and offers ready-to-use advice. She is also the founder and CEO of Compaas, a software vendor specializing in the analysis and management of compensation data. If you are beyond a couple of hundred employees and struggle with the complexity of your compensation data, you might want to check out this tool.

Easy on the Carrots:
Using Individual Incentives Effectively

EXECUTIVE SUMMARY: *Financial incentives are designed to influence employee behaviors in three ways. They help people decide if they want to work at your firm (selection effect), they tell employees what is important (information effect), and they can motivate people to try harder (motivation effect). Yet be careful what you reward! There are 8 conditions in which monetary rewards are effective, but they only rarely apply. Thus, go easy on the carrots. Sales is likely the only area where incentives work well and can be tailored to the psychological profiles of your stars, core performers, and laggards.*

Egon Zehnder:
"Deliberately Old-fashioned"

Egon Zehnder International, one of the world's largest executive search firms, was founded in Zürich, Switzerland, in 1964, a time when compensation in professional services was tied to seniority, not performance. While the executive search industry abandoned this model for performance-based schemes decades ago, Zehnder held on to this old-fashioned way of paying. Zehnder does not pay any kind of performance bonus – none. There is not even a formal procedure for tracking the performance of its 63 offices, let alone individuals.

Consultants receive a fixed salary while partners receive a share of the company's profits on top of that. Ten to 20 percent of profits are reinvested. The remaining 80-90 percent are distributed with two different parameters: 60 percent on a per-head basis and 40 percent based on the tenure of the partner (up to 15 years of tenure; after that, the bonus is the same). "At the close of a given year, for instance, a 10-year partner in any office will receive a larger share of the firm's profits than a five-year partner in any other office, even if the first office lost money and the second office broke billing records, thanks entirely to the five-year partner's billings," writes founder Egon Zehnder in an *HBR* article from 2001.

The main rationale behind this seemingly dated approach is to foster tight cooperation among the global network of over 500 consultants and the long-term view that Zehnder adopted as a core element of its strategy. Trusted, long-term relationships between client and consultant are key in the executive search business, and Zehnder makes every effort to create these. For Zehnder, a consultant becomes truly valuable after a decade of service when he or she knows the culture and inner workings of dozens of companies and can match the right candidate quickly and correctly.

In that sense, Zehnder nicely built out the logical chain depicted in the diagram on page 20 in Chapter 1. It uses its unique compensation system to convert a customer preference/differentiating activity (long-serving consultants who know the client, trustful, personal relationships) into cultural values (long-term approach to business) and consistent behavior of employees (investing time in relationships instead of chasing the next deal; loyalty to the firm).

Zehnder's recruiting approach supports this strategy, as well. The company looks for consultants with two characteristics: First, people who are in it for the long haul and don't mind spending their entire career at the company (the turnover among partners is 2 percent vs. the 30 percent industry average). Second, and in line with the profit-sharing approach, Zehnder prefers individuals who are team players, people who get more pleasure from the group's success than self-aggrandizement. Afraid that a "selling attitude" could contaminate its culture, Zehnder does not even interview consultants who have worked under a commission-based model in other search firms.

The story of Zehnder shows again how psychological, strategic, and often-counterintuitive compensation can be. Zehnder decides to be deliberately old-fashioned. The firm could do what everybody else in the industry does and pay its people fat bonuses. Yet this would be foolish, given the firm's culture and strategy. Financial incentives are difficult to design in a fast-changing world, and it is hard to maintain their effectiveness. Thus, we suggest you go *easy on the carrots* and check thoroughly if variable pay is your best option to provoke the desired behavior. This chapter will help you determine if and how financial incentives will work in your situation.

Making Individual Incentives Work

Variable pay, as opposed to base pay, needs to be re-earned each pay period. According to a study by WorldatWork, more than 90 percent of companies offer some sort of variable pay to their people, even though these schemes represent only a small portion of total compensation (5 percent in the US). Short-term incentives can be linked to the performance of an individual or a group. We will cover individual incentives and the special case of compensation of sales teams in this chapter. Group incentives will be treated in Chapter 4.

Three Effects of Financial Incentives

Financial incentives are offered to influence an employee's behavior. This can happen via three separate effects, as Jeffrey Pfeffer and Robert Sutton explain in their essay "Do Financial Incentives Drive Company Performance?"

Selection Effect ("Do I want to work here?"): Financial rewards are a cultural element that should attract the right and repel the wrong people. An aggressive, piece-rate compensation plan like Lincoln Electric's will attract individualist personalities who can stand pressure and don't mind a sportive competition among peers. In contrast, the straight salaries without bonuses or commissions at Egon Zehnder will appeal to people who feel more comfortable cooperating and working in teams.

Information Effect ("Do what is important"): Employees are exposed to a myriad of often contradictory messages and have difficulties separating the signal from the noise. A financial incentive can provide a clear signal. It tells employees that the company cares about a specific result. The logic goes: If they are willing to pay for this, then it must be important and deserves my attention.

Motivation Effect ("Try harder"): The most prevalent motive for offering people financial incentives is to make them work harder. Here the thesis goes that people will only give their very best effort if you offer them a reward.

While this third effect sounds like common sense and is practiced all over the world, the thesis has been seriously questioned by influential motivation theorists like Maslow (pyramid of needs), Herzberg (motivator-hygiene factor), or Deci & Ryan (cognitive evaluation theory). According to their research, financial rewards have little or no influence on work performance and can even be detrimental. Even though the original research is decades old, the theories have been popularized more recently by authors like Alfie Kohn (*Punished by Rewards*), Dan Pink (*Drive*), and Jeffrey Pfeffer (*Human Equation*) – and with considerable impact among business leaders.

Admittedly, we struggled to make sense of this discussion as it seems that the verdict is still pending. However, what we can conclude from this debate is the following: A wealth of research has shown that financial rewards can have a positive effect on performance. Large meta-studies show strong correlations between financial incentives and the results of people's work. Hence, for us, there is no question if financial incentives work. The question is rather how they work and *how* they can best be applied in practice.

Unwanted "Side Effects" of Incentive Schemes

And this is precisely the point where Kohn, Pink, Pfeffer, and others have enriched the debate. None of these authors claim categorically that incentives don't work. They rather point to a series of conditions that are required for them to be effective. Unfortunately, and in contrast to what many business leaders think, these conditions are only rarely found in the modern business world. Hence, designing financial incentive systems needs to be done with great care and consideration. In-appropriately applied incentive schemes can have multiple "side effects" that sabotage the original intentions as corporate scandals at Enron, Tyco, Wells Fargo, and the 2008 financial crisis have demonstrated.

> *"It is difficult to get a man to understand something when his salary depends on his not understanding it."*
> *- Upton Sinclair*

Let's review the most important ones:

Too Much of a Good Thing... is a bad thing. If the incentive system is the only guidance, some employees might keep pushing for the goal, ignoring other significant job duties. Bus drivers in some countries in Asia, rewarded for punctuality, drive by a bus stop full of people during rush hour, so they receive their punctuality bonus. Commissioned retail clerks neglect to stock up inventory and to take care of displays because they are overly focused on selling.

Too Complex but not Enough – Financial incentives carry information that affects people's choices. But only if the model is sufficiently simple to be understood by the employee. On the other hand, a too-simple model ignores relevant variables and will not deliver optimal results. The right balance is rarely achieved. Dan Cable recounts a study of British fertility clinics where a seemingly obvious and unambiguous performance goal – the percentage of pregnancies that result from treatment – turned out to be flawed and did not account for important long-term consequences. Clinics that focused on this metric ended up excluding women with complex medical conditions, which in turn deprived the clinics of valuable learning opportunities and limited their long-term perspectives (not to mention the ethical question of turning down desperate couples for purely economic reasons).

Cooking the Books – When tasks are modestly complex, it is impossible to anticipate every possible way that people might find to obtain their goals. Retail clerks hide popular items from colleagues to sell them when they are back from their break. Operators at a packaging facility for frozen peas bring insect pieces from home so they can "find" them and be financially rewarded. CEOs backdate options to make a killing. The tendency to find "creative" solutions increases with the size of the prize.

Performance Measures Tainted by Biases – A fundamental challenge with incentive systems (but also merit-pay) is to measure performance objectively. Jobs where the output is the exclusive merit of one person and can be accurately measured are very rare. Especially for knowledge workers, this is often impossible. Among other things, this is because the perception of what good performance looks like and how it should be rewarded can be very different for managers and employees (While 73 percent of employers consider their employees as paid fairly, only 36 percent of employees share that opinion, according to a study by PayScale). Another study shows that not even those who are objectively well paid by market standards perceive themselves as such.

Yet the main reasons for this mismatch are psychological biases. According to a study by Dunning, Heath, and Suls, ninety-seven percent of executives believe they are among the top 10 percent of performers. And

"...97 percent of executives believe they are among the top 10 percent of performers"

60 percent of a performance evaluation can be explained by attributes of the appraiser, not the appraisee, as Marcus Buckingham found out! Further issues arise when managers or peers give more lenient performance reviews because they know that their evaluation affects their co-worker's pay. So, even if the incentive works perfectly, you might not reward what you intended to because your performance metric measures something else.

Eight Conditions for Successful Incentives Schemes

These are some of the reasons why incentive schemes fail so regularly in practice. They don't fail because the incentives as such don't work, or people generally don't care about money. They fail because they are very difficult to design and implement properly. They fail because they produce the above "side effects." Hence, your best chance to avoid these issues is to limit the use of financial incentives to those situations where these side effects don't appear, i.e., when the following conditions are met:

1. The role is repetitive and focuses on doing just one thing.

2. The goals are unambiguous and one-dimensional.

3. It is easy to measure both the quantity and quality of results.

4. The employee has complete end-to-end control of process and outcome.

5. Cheating or gaming the results are practically impossible.

6. The role is very independent, i.e., there is little or no need for teamwork or collaboration.

7. The employee is not expected to help or support others.

8. The employee considers the incentive as meaningful, and the payout happens frequently.

The late Stanford economist Edward Lazear reports an impressive case study of the windshield repair company Safelite that switched from an hourly rate to a piece rate and harvested a 44 percent productivity gain. The incentive was effective in this case because the above conditions were met: Installing windshields is easy to learn and repetitive, goals were clear and results easily measurable (number of installed windshields). The work can be done independently, and the reward was significant ($20 per shield).

It's interesting to note that 50 percent of the productivity gain was due to the increased output of existing workers (motivational effect). The other 50 percent was attributable to less productive workers being replaced by more productive ones (selection effect).

Another example of a simple but effective incentive scheme from our community is Arnie Malham's *Better Book Club*. Arnie is the founder of CJ Advertising, an agency specialized in marketing for the legal profession. Arnie is a learning junkie and avid reader and wants his employees to read as well. So, he created a company library with over 400 books and assigned a point value to each book. After reading and completing a one-page book report, the employee receives a dollar per point. In total, 153 participating employees shared roughly $10,000 per year in bonuses – not a lot of money but enough to have thousands of books read by Arnie's team. To manage the program, Arnie created a system that is now available for any firm to use. Check out *www.betterbookclub.com*

Clear and simple conditions like these at Safelite or the Better Book Club have become less and less frequent in the modern service and information economy. Even if you enjoy them at a given moment, the context changes, and the schemes become outdated. This was the case for Sebastian and his team at TMC in 2015. After years of paying out unreasonable bonuses based on ill-designed and outdated incentive schemes, TMC abolished all individual and group incentives (the only exception is the sales team) and tied 80 percent of everybody's bonus to the company's financial performance (essentially a profit-sharing scheme, topic of Chapter 5) and the achievement of some tangible objectives, related to the quarterly theme (a gain-sharing scheme which we will introduce in Chapter 4).

"Our bonus schemes ended up being more of a problem than a solution. They produced unreasonable and unfair payouts for certain people and caused serious conflicts of objectives between departments. Rather than continuously adapt schemes and fight over objectives, we just put everybody in the same boat," shares TMC's People & Values Director Robert Van Tuijl. "Not everybody was happy with the change, but coherence and simplicity are of great value as well."

And TMC is in good company. German engineering giant Bosch eliminated all individual bonuses for its 378,000 employees in 2015. "The bonus at the end of the year will depend solely on how successful the company was. If things go well for Bosch, our people will benefit accordingly," says Bosch CEO Volkmar Denner. Other rockstar companies like Netflix, Mayo Clinic, or SAS Institute never had any performance bonuses.

> *"In today's economy, financial incentives do not drive performance. The carrot-and-stick approach is in fact often counterproductive. Financial incentives still have a role to play – as long as they are not expected to motivate people."*
>
> *– Hubert Joly, former Best Buy CEO and author of* The Heart of Business

Our general message here and the name of our third design principle is to *Go Easy on the Carrots*. This refers, in particular, to the motivation effect (the information and selection effect work more reliably, as we will see in Chapters 4 and 5). It is very difficult to obtain people's discretionary efforts for longer periods by dangling "carrots" in front of their faces. Check carefully if the job at hand meets the eight criteria outlined above. Your sales department might be the only place where that's the case (see next section). If not, then don't expect your people to work any harder and brace yourself for plenty of undesired "side effects."

Incentivizing Your Sales Team

Given its widespread use in sales departments, one could assume that variable pay is an effective formula to incentivize a sales force. According to compensation guru David Chichelli, eighty percent of sales teams have variable pay components, and the variable parts constitute around 40 percent of their total compensation. Practically every book on sales and sales compensation recommends the use of incentives for sales teams.

Do Financial Incentives Work in Sales?

Or rather the question is do they work *better* in sales? Authors like Dan Pink and David Hoffeld object and claim that financial incentives are just as useless for sales jobs as for any other occupation. They suggest leaders foster intrinsic and not extrinsic motivation. If someone doesn't have a natural drive to sell and needs an incentive, then they shouldn't be in sales in the first place, goes their argument.

There is research that supports both schools of thought. Countless studies provide evidence that financial incentives can significantly enhance sales performance. Other investigations demonstrate and explain the failure and overuse of such models.

One explanation for the confusion is that the sales function is changing at a rapid pace. Sales are becoming less transactional and more complex. Through the Internet, customers are well informed about the basic attributes of products and services. What they need are trustworthy and creative advisors who understand their situation and help them tailor solutions. Many salespeople nowadays sell *insights* rather than *items*. At the same time, sales organizations have become increasingly complex, with multiple agents and channels involved in the process (online, distributors, partners, telesales, sales engineers, key accounts, feet-on-street, etc.). In these situations, salespeople are rather the orchestrators of the process than the sole person responsible for the sale. Objectively measuring their individual performance is close to impossible and thus the difficulty to fairly compensate them for it.

In such a context, extrinsic motivation via financial incentives will not work, and companies need to fuel intrinsic motivation in any way they can. Intrinsic motivation is much more powerful and sustainable than extrinsic motivation. Excellence cannot be achieved without it. And for some sales organizations, this is all you need. SAS Institute is a case in point.

No Sales Incentives at SAS

SAS Institute, the North Carolina-based data analytics software house with 14,000 employees and a revenue of $3.1 billion, never even considered sales commissions because it is just not in its DNA. One of its four *basic principles* (their term for core values) is to "rely on intrinsic motivation." If you treat people with trust and respect, they'll be motivated to do a good job, which is SAS's working hypothesis. The other principle at odds with commissions is "Always think long term." Commissions can incite a sales rep to act against the long-term interest of the client and jeopardize the relationship. "We have sales targets, but mostly as a way of keeping score. I want to make the numbers the right way … I'm not smart enough to incent on a formula. People are constantly finding holes in incentive plans," says Barret Joyner, former head of North American Sales and Marketing at SAS. In general, SAS has a culture that consciously avoids the compensation topic. Since the very beginning, 45 years ago, founder James Goodnight avoided attracting people with money, so that they also don't leave for money. And this has always included salespeople (more on this unusual firm in Chapter 5).

It is obvious that sales commissions don't fit with a culture like SAS's. However, there are situations where it can be beneficial to support people's internal drive with a well-designed incentive plan. Plenty of sales jobs meet many or even all of the eight conditions listed above.

50% Sales Commissions

A Los Angeles-based home-automation company (you will understand in a moment why it wants to remain anonymous) presents such a case in point, as Dan Caulfield, executive sales coach at Jack Daly's coaching practice, shared with us. The company offers state-of-the-art automation technology for luxury homes, including entertainment, lighting, climate, security, communication, etc. The firm grew from $9.8 million to $20 million in revenue in six months due to slight twists in its business model, accompanied by relevant changes in its compensation schemes.

Expensive home-automation projects are generally put out for a bid by the homeowner or the construction company. When the 75-person company engaged with Dan Caulfield, the team was winning 35 percent of the jobs on which it bid but spending a lot of time on the bidding process. Then, at Caulfield's suggestion, the automation company introduced a new program. The sales team started selling prospects *Design Services Agreements (DSAs)* to help them "Love

Where They Live." The plans cost $1 per square foot. "The idea was that before you put this out to bid, you really need to know what it is you want and have a plan," says Caulfield. Given that most of the homes were about 12,000 square feet, the cost of the plans was comparatively low for prospects willing to spend, on average, $600,000 on home automation at the time. To incentivize the sales team to sell these design studies, half of the revenue from the study would go to them. So, for instance, if the plan for a 12,000-square-foot house costs the customer $12,000, the sales rep would get $6,000.

Many of the prospects loved the idea of purchasing a design services agreement, says Caulfield. It helped them determine what they wanted. Although the owners were free to bid out the jobs to any contractor they wanted on the completion of the plan, almost everybody opted to simply continue with the existing team.

"We went from a sales cycle being six, nine, or 12 months long to the very first time we met with the customer we'd come home with a signed piece of paper and check," says Caulfield. "Salespeople wouldn't have to wait for 18-20 months for a project to be done to be commissioned and paid." And with customers clear on what they wanted from their home-automation program, the average size of each job jumped to close to $1 million.

With the additional income from the DSA, the conversion rate went up from 35 percent to practically 100 percent, and because of the increased commission from the bigger job size, salespeople earned 1.5x to 3x more in six months than they made in the entire previous year on the old commission program, according to Caulfield. Yes, the commission was high by industry standards, but there was no wasted work on bidding, saving the company more than $400,000 per year.

This case shows again how strategic compensation decisions can be. Without the 50 percent commission on the income from the design study, sales reps might have just continued to sell the entire installation project, and the company might have never discovered this magic formula.

Conclusion: Yes, incentives work in sales, even better than in most other functions. Intrinsic motivation is a requirement for a sales role but is often not enough to develop the full potential of your sales force. Thus, for many sales teams, it does make sense to additionally motivate people with monetary incentives. Extrinsic and intrinsic motivation are complementary for a sales force.

Seven Design Elements of a Sales Compensation Plan

A professional sales force requires a documented sales compensation plan where you define *who* gets paid *when* and for *what*. The best sources of advice on how to design such a plan are David Cichelli's book *Compensating the Sales Force* and Chad Albrecht's and Steve Marley's book *The Future of Compensation* – the former for a deep understanding of the fundamentals and practicalities of sales compensation, the latter for an outlook on how sales compensation is evolving (analytics, technology, gamification, personalization, millennials) and how you can anticipate these changes. This section draws heavily on Chapter two of *Compensating the Sales Force*, where Cichelli distinguishes the following seven design elements of a sales compensation plan.

1. Eligibility

First, you define who is eligible for your compensation plan. A common criterion is if people influence the customer's purchase decision or not. The plan might include the telesales team but exclude field engineers.

2. Target Total Cash Compensation

Next, you obtain benchmarks for the total target cash compensation (TTCC) and decide where you want to position yourself. What should top performers make, compared to the market (50th, 75th, or 90th percentile?). What should laggards take home? (more on market references in Appendix D).

3. Pay Mix and Leverage

If you believe that incentives are beneficial for your sales force, then you need to decide on the percentage of TTCC you want to put at risk for your people. Any variable compensation must reflect the inherent risk of the job (territory, product, accounts, competition, etc.). Most compensation plans are too flat. The target incentive should have a weight of at least 15 percent to be significant and effective as an incentive.

The higher the influence of the sales rep over the purchasing decision, the bigger the variable component can be. Nike, for example, pays a sales commission of only 15 percent on large strategic accounts like Decathlon, in which many Nike departments are involved in the sales process, vs. 30-50 percent for sales to small shops in rural areas where a single sales rep manages the entire process.

The *leverage* of a compensation plan defines its upside potential (see the figure below). Many plans are designed in a way that top performers can make three times the target incentive. But don't cap the plan at 3x. Research shows that caps don't save you money but rather make you lose potential revenue and profit. Stars want to be rewarded as such. Salary dispersion is of less concern on sales teams because performance can be measured more objectively. The causality is clear, and people consider pay differences as acceptable – given that territory, product mix, etc., offer equal opportunities.

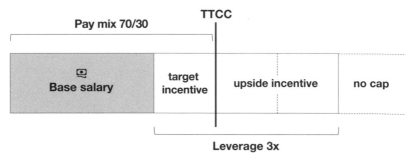

Pay mix and leverage

4. Performance Measures and Weight

Defining performance measures and weights is where your compensation systems start to drive strategy. Performance measures can be classified by the object of measurement:

1. Volume production (revenue, margin, profit, # items)
2. Sales effectiveness (product mix, account mix, price)
3. Customer impact (customer loyalty or satisfaction, contribution to core purpose)
4. Resource utilization (productivity, channel mix, team implication)

Or by the phase of the sales cycle:

1. Customer identification and solicitation–finding the potential buyer
2. Demand creation–introducing and presenting the value proposition
3. Point of persuasion–moving customers to the purchase commitment
4. Delivering the product–ensuring the value proposition is fulfilled
5. Servicing the order–ensuring the value proposition is sustained

Where you put the focus depends on your strategy and execution constraints. Choose a maximum of three measures and assign them a weight. An individual weight should not be lower than 15 percent. Variable pay should be based on margin, not revenue. You want a profitable business and not any business. If margins are not an option (e.g., because it can't be predicted reliably), then the sales rep shouldn't have control over prices.

5. Quota Distribution

A quota is an individual sales target assigned to a salesperson. It is a required minimum for a given period. Setting quotas is a delicate act. If quotas are too low, you are overpaying the sales force. If they are too high, you are cheating them. A good quota distribution is when two-thirds of sales reps achieve their quota, and one-third fails. Quotas need to be adjusted from time to time but increasing quotas of your top performers every year ("ratcheting") is perceived as unfair and is detrimental to performance.

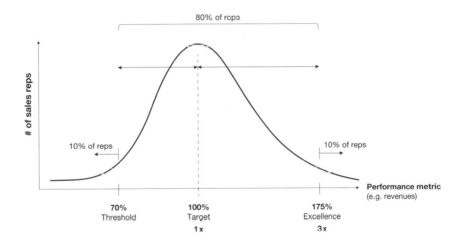

Quota distribution and performance range

6. Performance Range

The performance range defines for each measure (e.g., revenue, # items sold, productivity) the lower threshold of performance where you start paying commission and the highest level you can reasonably expect (e.g., 3x leverage). For a mature business with stable sales, you could decide to pay variable starting at a quota level of 85 percent and position the maximum at 115 percent. For a new product, a 175 percent over the target level might be possible and can be rewarded with 3x the target incentive. Depending on whether the upside is capped or not, the payout can be more than 3x. 80 percent of sales reps should perform within the range between minimum and maximum level.

7. Performance and Payment Periods

The last item to define is the length of the period for which you measure performance (week, month, quarter, year) and the frequency with which you pay out the variable compensation. These two periods are normally identical, but it is important to define if these periods are cumulative or discrete. Discrete means that each period counts for itself, and performance and payout are not affected by preceding or subsequent periods. Cumulative means that the sales force receives proportionally smaller quarterly payouts at the beginning of the period, which will then be set off against a total year-end payment. This system runs the danger of procrastination but is also motivating in low periods because it gives the rep the chance to make up for bad quarters.

Stars, Core Performers, and Laggards

A way to optimize your sales compensation plan is by tailoring its features to the psychological profiles of your *stars*, core *performers*, and *laggards*, as professors Steenburgh and Ahearne call these three groups in an *HBR* article titled "Motivating Salespeople: What Really Works," which we recommend you read.

Stars need unlimited upside potential. They call it a day once they have maxed out. For them, commissions should be uncapped and accelerate once they have reached their quota. In general, research shows that frugality toward top salespeople doesn't pay off.

Core performers hit their targets but rarely exceed them. Multi-tier targets with increasing payouts help them as steppingstones up the performance curve. The typical sales contest doesn't work well for core performers because they never win.

Laggards need intermittent goals, frequent touchpoints with management, quarterly bonus payouts (ideally cumulative), and pressure from upcoming "bench" players who compete for their territories.

Dell offers an example of such customization. The computer manufacturer faced a challenge when they first moved from just selling hardware to complete integration solutions. Because the latter was more time consuming and difficult, even the best salespeople opted for the quick, lower margin, hardware sale. To counter this, Dell identified their highly commissioned "stars" and limited them to nine deals per year! This had a powerful "information effect" on these top performers, strongly directing them to go for the massive and more complex sales opportunities. And it worked.

Structural changes to the comp systems, like those at Dell, can be disruptive for the sales team and lead to anxiety and demotivation. Steve Hall, founder and former CEO of DriverSelect, a large Dallas-based nearly-new car retailer (now part of the EchoPark Group), found a creative solution to this problem. Six months before introducing any new comp scheme, Hall dry runs the new plan in parallel with the existing plan and gathers data on how it changes an employee's income. Based on these outcomes, together with training and coaching, the agents have time to adjust their sales approach and avoid income losses. Moreover, during the last two of the six-month dry run period, Hall gives his reps the option to be paid under the new or the old plan, whichever was more favorable to them at the end of the month.

Competing with Larger Firms

Smaller firms often have difficulties competing with larger competitors in terms of base salary and benefits. But they can make up for the difference, especially if they are growing, by generously sharing the upside with their people.

That's what Tim Brady, CEO of Vancouver-based Colligo compliance and governance software, does. He pays under-market on base salary but over-market on commission and bonus. Account executives, for example, once they have earned their base salary, get 20 percent on every sale with no cap. "This makes our top-performers very well paid and stick around," shares Brady.

By the way, the scheme is also well aligned with Colligo's core value of "acting like an owner." To model this ownership thinking, Brady himself takes the lowest base salary in the company. Brady knows he'll make serious money if his employees do as well.

Sales compensation is an ample topic, and this section only scratched the surface. If you run a sizable sales team or plan to scale one over the coming years, then we recommend you study David Cichelli's book *Compensating the Sales Force*. It is a must-read, loaded with useful structure and practical tips that will help make your sales team even more successful.

Evolving Compensation Along
the Growth Cycle

The story of Tinuiti (formerly EliteSEM), a digital performance marketing firm headquartered in New York City, shows how the incentive system can play a key role in scaling a company but also the need to evolve the system with the company's growth and changes in strategy. Founded in 2004, Tinuiti has used its compensation system as a strategic driver for its rapid growth (50 percent compound annual growth for the last 16 years – in part through acquisitions) and today has more than 700 employees in nine offices around the US.

Digital marketing is an extremely dynamic field where new technologies continuously change the landscape. Attracting the very best talent is key in such an environment. "Our hyper growth would not have happened without our bespoke compensation system," says Zach Morrison, CEO of Tinuiti.

The system has evolved since then, but back in its early years, the company offered an almost all variable and uncapped compensation as a strategy to attract qualified professionals that could accelerate growth. Essentially anyone in a client-facing role (then 90 percent of the team) took part in a comp system that awarded points for each gross margin dollar generated. "We were small and did not have much to show for in terms of employer brand and benefits. But our compensation system got people's attention and had a strong signaling effect among ambitious young people willing to work very hard for exceptional pay," explains Morrison.

New employees were put on a fixed salary for 18 months to learn the ropes but then got the option: They could either stay on the fixed salary or join the point system with unlimited upside but also a very low floor. "Interestingly, nobody ever took the fixed salary," reports Morrison. This quite aggressive way of sharing profit was the company's way of kick-starting the hyper-growth phase that took them from 14 employees in 2011 to now more than 700.

The situation today is different, and the firm has evolved its comp system accordingly. Tinuiti is now much more established and can offer a well-rounded reward package with less emphasis on pay. As a result, the company has received a long list of accolades for the attractiveness of its workplace and culture. *Fortune Magazine* recognized it for "Best Workplaces for Millennials" in 2016. It has a Glassdoor rating of 4.7 (out of 5), and CEO Zach Morrison enjoys a 93 percent approval rating on the review site. The astonishing employee Net Promoter Score (eNPS) of 77+ gives testimony to the great culture that Morrison and his team have created. "People now join us for our culture, development opportunities, and many other reasons, and we like that. Pay is still very attractive and up to 30-40 percent above industry average, but it is only one of several decision factors," shares Jennifer Garrison, SVP of People at Tinuiti and a winner of a Gold Stevie Business Award for Chief Human Resources Officer of the Year.

In the meantime, a larger and more diversified client base has reduced the business risk and thus the need to share this risk with employees. Tinuiti now offers a fixed base salary that matches average pay levels in the industry to all staff. On top of this, all client-facing staff (now 75 percent of all employees) continue with the point system that gives them a commission based on gross profit per client. The commission kicks in when clients reach a certain revenue threshold and can add up to an additional 30-40 percent onto the base pay. "This is less aggressive than it used to be but still provides our people with the highest compensation levels in the industry. We overpay our people, but at the same time we are hyper-focused on their happiness. The result is that they are more productive, and we still have higher-than-average industry margins," explains Morrison (Recognize the pattern? Another example of a highly effective Good Jobs Strategy.).

Remarkable that Tinuiti pays this incentive-based on group performance. Commissions are determined and paid out monthly based on client profitability. For a group of people working on a particular client, a profit share is determined and then distributed among the team members according to their job categories. A *Coordinator* gets a smaller share than the *Specialist*, a *Specialist* makes less than a *Strategist*, and so on. Department heads have the latitude to deviate from these default keys to reflect the real dedication to the client and any special merits in a given month.

Tinuiti's commission system meets only a few of the eight conditions of effective incentives systems we outlined above. Yet surprisingly, it works. It works, first, because the firm constantly twists and and tweaks the system to keep it functional. But it also works because Tinuity has complementary People practices in place that mitigate the risks of such an aggressive system. The rigorous selection process, the 18-month waiting period, good IT systems and data, and intensive training all assure that people are more concerned about growing the pie than fighting about the exact size of their piece.

Tinuiti's example illustrates another important point we want to make: Compensation is anything but an exact science. Human psychology is too complex to capture in universally valid formulas. Whether a given formula works or not highly depends on the context. As with Tinuiti's commission system, you can compensate a theoretical weakness of a system with other People practices and great leadership. Again, adapting your compensation system to your particular context is vital for success. This book provides general guidelines and hopefully will inspire you with examples. Yet, the precise winning formula for your incentives schemes (and your compensation systems as a whole) will only emerge as the result of experimentation and continuous learning in your particular context.

Thanks, in part, to the compensation system, Tinuiti has only a 10 percent voluntary turnover rate. "That is a 5 times better retention rate than our peers," Garrison says. That is a powerful competitive advantage (and confirms our claim in the sub-title of this book).

Gamify Gains:
Driving Critical Numbers Through P(l)ay

EXECUTIVE SUMMARY: *Shorter-term gain-sharing plans are used to gamify the business and add a level of fun and excitement (and dopamine addiction!) to achieving FAST (vs. SMART) goals. They help to drive a clearer focus and better decision-making throughout the organization. Further borrowing from the psychology employed by casinos, intermittent and surprise rewards can be the one type of compensation that is highly motivational, driving magnitude increases in results. Again, people are not logical; they are psychological. Design comp accordingly.*

MiniMovers:
"A Bonus for Not Breaking Stuff"

Breaking things is the quickest way to get in trouble at MiniMovers. Not with the customer or your boss. It is your teammates who will instantly pounce on you when you break a customer's item – way before the customer himself or your boss would ever notice. Why? Because MiniMovers runs an ingenious incentive scheme in which your pay depends on your coworkers' carefulness.

MiniMovers is a 36-year-old company headquartered in Brisbane, Australia, that specializes in door-to-door local moving, generating about AUD 30 million per year. The firm employs 450 movers in Australia and about 50 sales and back-office support workers in the Philippines.

It was the founder and managing director Mike O'Hagan who came up with the bonus scheme almost 25 years ago. Most moving companies pay expensive insurance policies to cover the risks of breakage. MiniMovers self-insures. It sets aside 3 percent of revenue for a team bonus that gets divided up among the movers and distributed every three months – if nothing is broken. If there is breakage, the company subtracts the cost of the damage from the breakage and uses the cash to reimburse its customers.

As a result, movers police themselves to make sure nothing gets broken. "If someone is not doing the right thing, the coworkers will quickly step in," says O'Hagan. "They will train new colleagues on the spot to make sure they are handling customers' property the right way."

The amount distributed to each team member can be significant – over AUD 1,000. "Quite often, it's enough to buy something like a flat-screen TV," says O'Hagan. "And it doesn't cost anything extra, from the company's point of view. But I prefer paying the 3 percent, or whatever is left at the end of the quarter, to our people, and not an insurance company."

"Staff tend to mortgage themselves to their income level, counting bonuses as if it's ALWAYS going to be there."

Another positive aspect of the scheme is that it avoids a common problem with bonuses: habituation. "Staff tend to mortgage themselves to their income level, counting bonuses as if it's ALWAYS going to be there," explains O'Hagan.

MiniMovers compensation program helps it retain a great workforce as well. "We pay well above the minimum wage," says O'Hagan, and the breakage bonus makes the overall package quite attractive. O'Hagen also makes sure his firm doesn't hire anyone with poor work habits picked up at other companies. MiniMovers recruits only from outside the industry and puts new joiners through its training program. "We will not hire anyone with a truck driver's license or if they've worked in our industry," says O'Hagan.

Effective Gain-sharing Schemes

O'Hagen's ingenious bonus program is what HR professionals would classify as gain-sharing. In a *gain-sharing* scheme, teams or even the entire company commit to moving the needle on what Jack Stack would call a *critical number*, i.e., a metric that points to a challenge of the business (productivity, spending, quality, customer service). This number is then tied to a bonus and paid out to employees when the goal is achieved. If you gamify the scheme, it will become even more effective. Because people engage and change their behavior purely to have fun, the monetary incentive becomes secondary or even irrelevant. That's why we called our fourth design principle *Gamify Gains*.

You can apply gain-sharing schemes as one-time thrusts to accomplish a particular objective and then move on to the next thing. Or, as in the case of

MiniMovers, they can be used to continuously focus the team's attention on a critical performance indicator (e.g., breakage). In fact, the program has been so successful in keeping team members focused on reducing breakage that O'Hagen can almost forget about a problem of epidemic dimensions for the rest of his industry. "The team members deal with it because it is coming out of their pockets," he says.

Gain-sharing plans use the information effect of incentives. By making goals specific and tangible, and tying a reward to them, gain-sharing plans tell people what is important. We find MiniMovers' plan particularly noteworthy because it is strategic in the sense that it uses an incentive to convert customer expectations (intact belongings) into consistent employee behavior (handling belongings with care).

The LA-based home-automation company we introduced in Chapter 3 offers a similarly ingenious example of a gain-sharing scheme that keeps a team focused on what is important.

Share the Last 10%

After having learned how to sell million-dollar projects through *Design Services Agreements*, Dan Caulfield, the sales coach we met earlier, also reinvented how these complex projects are delivered.

For that purpose, Caulfield introduced a "Happiness Guarantee" to clients and tied this guarantee to a significant group incentive for the installation team. Prospects who decided to hire the home-automation company received the promise that the firm would guarantee their happiness 100 percent, or they would not have to pay the last 10 percent of the contract. If the clients do pay the last 10 percent, it is split equally between the 15 to 25 employees who interacted with the client.

Given the typical deal size of $600,000 to $1 million, everybody from planners to installers went out of their way to dazzle the customers and receive their share of the "tip." "Project managers drove all night to ensure everything was in place on move-in-day," says Caulfield. They would bring flowers or a bottle of wine when they came to show the clients how to use their equipment. "It aligned them directly with the happiness of the customers and was critical in driving referrals," says Caulfield.

Challenges of Group Incentives

Group incentives like the one at MiniMovers or the home-automation company can be highly effective but are not without challenges. Group incentives have the advantage of fostering collaboration and teamwork. They tend to be the better option when work is highly interdependent and you have a collaborative culture. But in general, group incentives suffer from the same side effects of individual incentives that we described earlier (movers could work too slowly to avoid breaking things; the costs for the home-automation projects could get out of hand if employees do "whatever" to please the customer; Tinuiti's marketing specialists could manipulate data to improve margins, etc.), plus they have their own set of drawbacks:

First, most people don't want to depend on others when it comes to their pay. Second, top performers are the least fond of group schemes as they cross-subsidize weaker performers and make them earn less (one study found that given a choice, high performers chose the individual system, whereas low performers chose the group incentive system). This can provoke a negative selection effect when highly productive people leave the company and others refrain from joining because of such group schemes. Third, the free-rider effect (people slack because they trust that others will carry their load) can bring average performance down instead of up – a problem that increases with team size.

However, there are situations where tight cooperation within a team is required, and group incentives create a healthy dose of peer pressure that leads to improved performance, as in the case of the breakage bonus at MiniMovers or the Happiness Guarantee that Dan Caufield invented.

If you use such gain-sharing schemes, make sure that individual performance is monitored as well. Otherwise, free riders might ruin morale, top performers could desert, and overall performance could come down and not up. Hybrid incentive models that reward individual *and* group performance theoretically avoid this, but their complexity is often prohibitive and produces the side effects mentioned above.

A way to reduce unintended side effects of group incentives is to link rewards to metrics that reflect the overall performance of the organization, like company profit. But you can apply the same logic to other aggregated goals that the entire company shoots for in joint gain-sharing exercises. Here is an impressive example that illustrates the power that such schemes can exert.

$100,000 for Everyone

Hilcorp is a Houston, Texas-based oil and natural gas producer, founded in 1989 and today the largest privately-owned extraction company in the United States. Jeffrey Hildebrand, the company's founder, built the firm by purchasing discarded assets from major oil and gas companies and using his superior technology to extract more oil and gas from these assets than the large companies could.

Yet it is not only extraction technology that makes this company successful. Hildebrand has also been doing a phenomenal job in motivating his people, today more than 3,100. The firm has been on Best Companies to Work For lists since 2015 (#70 nationwide on Fortune's Top 100 in 2020), so it must get a few things right with employees. However, what caught our attention is a stunning gain-sharing scheme the firm introduced in 2006.

That year, Jeffrey Hildebrand launched the *DoubleDrive* campaign – a gain-sharing plan that promised to pay all employees a $50,000 voucher toward a car if the oil-field production rate and its net oil and gas reserves doubled by 2010. The team met the goal, and, at the beginning of 2011, Hilcorp shelled out $35 million to its employees. "We always want to set it up so when Hilcorp wins, everyone wins," said CEO Greg Lalicker, then president. "Our people know it's not just for some faceless, nameless shareholder's benefit. We're doing it for the benefit of all 700 employees."

Directly after achieving this "surreal" goal, Hildebrand launched the *Dream 2015* campaign, doubling the reward to $100,000 if the team could again double net production and reserves by 2015. To the astonishment of the business community, at the beginning of 2016, 1,400 employees received a $100,000 check.

The hefty bonus and the fact that everybody receives the same amount, from receptionist to CEO, speaks volumes about Hilcorp's culture and its sense of fairness. But the story also illustrates the powerful information effect that well-designed gain-sharing schemes can have. We doubt that Hilcorp's employees worked consistently harder over the long decade that these plans were playing out. But we are sure that the outsized bonuses made them make better decisions and set different priorities. And this is not a one-time effect. Organizational learning is an important by-product of gain-sharing schemes. People understand causalities and make better decisions because of these plans.

Axiometrics – Rocks Logic

Scaling Up practitioners will appreciate that gain-sharing schemes are also great ways to reinforce a firm's annual or quarterly priorities ("rocks" in our language). That's how Axiometrics, a Dallas-based big data company in the real estate space, implemented its gain-sharing plan. According to Keith Walters, president and COO from 2012 until its sale in 2017 and a long-time Scaling Up evangelist, the gain-sharing plan was key in scaling the firm at a 40 percent annual growth rate and eventually selling it for $75 million to a publicly-traded company.

Walters tied everybody's compensation to the achievements of the firm's three annual priorities. Team members received a percentage of base salary when hitting the target for each priority. "If we came under target, there was under-payment and sometimes nothing because we also had cliffs," Walters shared. "For over-target achievements, we had a rachet that generated overpayment, i.e., 110 percent of achievement generated a 125 percent payout."

Axiometrics' priorities were operationalized through FAST goals (**F**requently-discussed, **A**mbitious, **S**pecific, **T**ransparent – an update to the acronym SMART goals). Priorities included customer retention, revenue per employee, and percentage of total real estate stock covered. Walters' team tracked each variable constantly so that everyone could see if they were on plan or not. Team members also had a spreadsheet that allowed them to calculate their individual expected payouts at any time. The real payout at Axiometrics was quarterly yet based upon YTD performance so that late performance could catch up with early non-performance.

 WARNING: *Don't get carried away with sophisticated schemes that have multiple and weighted goals, floors, caps, and all sorts of other covenants. Simplicity is essential for these plans to work.*

Another example of a simple yet highly effective gain-sharing scheme is Continental Airlines' punctuality bonus, introduced in 1995. All employees, from CEO to flight attendant, received an additional $65 with their monthly paycheck if the airline ranked in the top five for on-time performance the previous month. The campaign was hugely successful. "We made it into the top three for punctuality and transformed a $615 million loss into a $224 million win in one year, among other items, because we avoided paying $6 million per month to re-accommodate passengers on competitor's flights," explains Greg Brenneman, COO of Continental during the turnaround.

It wasn't the size of the bonus that mattered as much as the focus it brought to the airline's on-time performance. Because of the high interdependence between the different jobs in an airline, peer pressure and solidarity had a big impact on the success of this initiative as well.

In a similar fashion, Sebastian at TMC paid a small bonus (=0.5 percent of annual salary) to everybody when the team achieved the goals of the quarterly theme. Again, it wasn't the money that moved people to put in the extra effort but rather the game-like spirit these schemes created. Read up on quarterly themes in Verne's book *Scaling Up (Rockefeller Habits 2.0)* if you don't work with them yet. They are a powerful way of rallying the troops around a common objective and getting stuff done.

 KEY RESOURCE: *If you are interested in implementing gain-sharing schemes, read Chapter 7 in Jack Stack's book* Great Game of Business *and learn how to design a program that gets your team excited. Jack's company, SRC Holdings Corporation, also has an educational wing that offers courses on open-book management and the Great Game of Business approach to management. Send a team to Springfield, Missouri, to attend a two-day "Get in the Game" workshop. It's particularly useful for CFOs and COOs. Seeing is believing.*

Irregular, Ad Hoc Rewards

Using financial and non-financial rewards in an irregular, ad hoc matter is an excellent tactic to increase the motivational effect and avoid the creation of entitlements. Research and practice have shown that compensation works best as a motivator when it comes right after the desired behavior. Computer games make extensive use of this effect. Annual bonuses and merit-based raises are less effective because too much time goes by.

Paul Berman, CEO of Philadelphia-area id8 Strategies, a digital marketing agency, has experienced excellent results with surprise bonuses. "Raises do little to improve performance or motivation," notes Berman. "What I have read and experienced is that within two weeks, the enjoyment of slightly higher income fades away."

"On the other hand, surprise bonuses are fun and tie into the one-minute manager concept of catching people doing the right thing and handing out a nice bonus," exclaims Berman. The size of the bonus – normally $500 to $1,000 – depends on the person and their role. And not all are cash. Other types include sports tickets, something special for their family, a kind gift or a combination.

"These surprise bonuses are one-time nonrecurring expenses," concludes Berman. "They help to build culture and have been highly effective for me for a long time."

In the same spirit, TMC introduced some years ago the *Invisible Hero Award*. Anybody can suggest a colleague they think has made an extraordinary contribution or effort. The suggestion is presented and decided informally at the weekly senior leadership meeting. The award can be anything from a dinner for two to a voucher to a material gift. The upper limit per award is $1,000.

The reward is not publicized, but the employee can, of course, share the news. Every time this reward is given (about once a month), people's reactions show how meaningful such a small and inexpensive gesture of appreciation can be. A colleague from the Barcelona office who had received a $200 dinner voucher wrote: "Thanks so much for this, I'm so pleased and touched to have been nominated. It's such an amazing reward. My wife and I are both looking forward to it so much."

Full Gamification

The casino industry best understands how to use what the clinical psychologist and bestselling author Aubrey Daniels calls *intermittent reinforcement schedules* to get people to lose their money! It's the thrill of not knowing the amount or the frequency – the surprise! – that makes gambling so thrilling and creates that dopamine addiction referenced earlier. And whereas companies struggle to get people to work late nights and weekends, it's not an issue for casinos. As such, why not put it to work for you?

Verne stumbled across this idea when he was asked to consult for the Home Shopping Network (HSN). The network had thousands of people working in their call centers, sitting and staring at screens much like people in casinos. One challenge was getting these call center reps to upsell. If someone purchased a necklace, all the agent needed to do was ask the buyer if they would like the matching bracelet. If the sale was made, a small "spiff" (commission) was earned.

The reps didn't even need to be that skilled at asking – they just had to ask. Yet almost all reps failed to ask for the additional sale. Why? All that needed to happen, once, was a customer screaming at the rep "If I wanted the f'ing bracelet, I would have asked for it," and the rep wasn't going to ever ask again. The small spiff just wasn't worth the embarrassment, so the commission money just sat there unspent.

So, Verne (partnering with Aubrey Daniels at the time) advised HSN to turn its call centers into casino-like environments. Instead of earning a consistent spiff, reps earned the right to spin a big wheel installed in each call center – giving them chances to win movie tickets, dinners, flat-screen TVs and even an automobile (HSN parked one outside the entrance to the call centers as a reminder) – just like casinos.

To everyone's surprise, upselling increased not just by 5, 10, or 20 percent – but a whopping 250 percent: same reps, same products, same total commission pool. The difference was the use of intermittent vs. constant reinforcement schedules – and the chance to win big!

Later Verne implemented a similar program with a small architectural steel and piping firm in the Boston area. With 60 employees, the owner had allocated $60,000 for bonuses. When calculating who received what bonus became a complicated distractor and demotivator, the owner used the money to gamify the business.

Allocating $5,000 per month, all employees who achieved individual or team goals that month had their name put in a bingo-style spinning machine. And if they exceeded their goals by a certain amount, their name was placed twice in the machine.

They would then gather in an all-hands meeting and spin the bingo machine. First, for small prizes like movie passes and dinners for two. If you won, you were disqualified from winning a second time that month. The grand prize was $2,000 in cash.

One month, Verne was present at the all-hands, and the winner was a colleague from the warehouse. When his name was announced, the entire warehouse team erupted into celebration. He came to find out that, like people pool resources to purchase lottery tickets, the five members of the warehouse team agreed to support each other in exceeding their individual and team goals so they would get the maximum 10 chances each month – and if anyone won the big cash prize, they would split it five ways!

The owner afterward shared that he had been trying to get the warehouse team to be more supportive and cooperative with each other, to no avail. Instead, his gamified bonus plan did the trick.

KEY RESOURCE: *Read Chapter 18 in Aubrey Daniels' book* Bringing Out the Best in People *to learn more about designing effective monetary and non-monetary reward systems.*

Non-Monetary Rewards

There is no need to always tie gain-sharing plans to a dollar amount. Non-monetary rewards come in countless forms: extra vacation days, sabbaticals, special projects, training or educational events (i.e., paying for a conference at an exotic location, including spouse or family), travel privileges (business class flight, 5-star hotel), or simply throwing a great party for your people.

Research indicates that non-monetary rewards have a more substantial impact on performance than monetary rewards of equivalent value. Part of the explanation is that non-monetary rewards, especially experience gifts (i.e., a trip or an educational event), evoke emotions in people, and emotions help memories stick. People won't remember the zeros on their bank statements, but they will never forget how you made them feel with that trip to Hawaii.

Paying for education is also more impactful than just handing over a check. Starbucks took that route and offers all its "partners" (their term for employee) to earn their bachelor's degree with full tuition coverage to graduation at Arizona State University's online degree program. Starbucks contributes between $9,000-$16,000 per partner until graduation in this program. All benefits-eligible partners working an average of 20 hours per week can participate, and there is no commitment to stay after graduation.

An innovative form of a non-monetary reward is an "altruistic" bonus. A team of researchers explored the impact of providing employees and teammates with a bonus they must spend on others rather than themselves. The study showed that spending money on others – whether coworkers or charity – increased the happiness and job satisfaction of givers *and* receivers and improved team performance.

Employee-directed Charity

Hilcorp, the Texan oil and gas company we met earlier, is not only outrageously generous to its employees. It is also top-notch when it comes to community contributions. The firm gives $2,500 to all new employees to donate to a non-profit organization of their choice upon hiring. From then on, Hilcorp matches every year, and dollar for dollar, the employees' donation to their favorite non-profit organizations – up to $2,000. Since its inception, Hilcorp's employees have donated over $18 million via this method. On top of donating, Hilcorp employees also volunteer their time in their local communities, and Hilcorp itself supports team members with children by providing educational scholarships. "At Hilcorp, we take a stand for what is right. We do the right thing, we give back, we help others. Not because we have to, but because it reflects who we are," is a quote from the firm's website.

Verne has been practicing a similar approach with his team at Scaling Up. In December, every team member receives $2,000 to give to the charities of their choice. Yes, many companies give to charity. But the twist of letting the employee choose the organization and deliver the money is crucial – the employee receives direct recognition by the charity for the gift instead of the company.

Chess vs. Checkers

The idea of non-monetary rewards also allows you to customize your compensation for specific employees – and aligns with Marcus Buckingham's notion that good leaders play checkers; great leaders play chess. You want a wide range of talents and often some individuals/teams require a unique approach to total rewards.

As Verne was scaling up his firm Gazelles (now called Scaling Up), he had a friend Rob who had sold his firm for a gazillion dollars and had some time and interest in helping him with technology needs. There was no way for Verne to pay Rob the kind of salary he was used to as the CEO of a significant technology firm. But Rob loved the challenge and surprisingly agreed to the much smaller salary that Gazelles could afford at the time.

After hurting his back while shoveling snow, and in recognition of a milestone Rob had just achieved (and feeling guilty over the low salary), Verne purchased Rob a snowblower. Verne later came to find out that Rob wouldn't spend money on himself, even though he was wealthy by modern standards. So, Verne structured his quarterly "bonuses" to reward Rob with gadgets he wanted but wouldn't buy for himself – something that was fun, strengthened their personal relationship, and led to many late-night conversations both still remember to this day.

This chapter provided plenty of practical examples of how companies creatively use gain-sharing schemes to influence people's behavior. What these plans all have in common is that they make good use of the information effect of incentives - often with the additional appeal of playing a game and have some fun. Peer accountability is another common success factor of these plans. Gain-sharing schemes can have a motivation effect (we can safely assume that the home-automation guys put in some extra hours to get the 10 percent happiness bonus), but research shows that it is less significant, less sustainable, and consequently shouldn't be the reason you offer these rewards.

In any case, in business practice, it is impossible to assess the precise effect of a particular incentive on people's behavior. Incentives can trigger a great variety of responses in people, and the exact causes of behavior changes are difficult to establish. Other variables like leadership, culture, or training influence heavily if a given compensation plan works or not. Again, the right formula for your organization requires experimentation and continuous adaption to changing circumstances.

Sharing Is Caring:
Getting Employees to Think Like Owners

EXECUTIVE SUMMARY: *Profit sharing is a question of fairness, with the added benefit of creating an ownership mentality throughout the organization. Like other forms of compensation, it is not necessarily a motivator, but it does influence the team's decisions positively – as long as it doesn't support "bad profits." Profit-sharing is also a way for mid-market firms to compete for talent. Longer-term value sharing (stock and stock options) goes even further in aligning the interests of owners and employees. It can create true wealth for your team and even eliminate a key constraint in your industry, as it did for Outback Steakhouse. Going public is an option worth considering, even for small firms. Phantom stock is a special form of value sharing that retains control for the owners but can create liquidity issues.*

Access Fixtures:
"No More Wining and Dining"

Steve Rothschild, co-founder and Senior Lighting Specialist (more on his title below) of Worchester, Massachusetts-based Access Fixtures, wanted all of his people to think like owners. For Rothschild, thinking like an owner means, for example, watching gross margins and not revenue. For an employee without skin in the game, any sale is a good sale. Yet, owners closely watch the margin they make on every sale.

To get his team thinking this way, Rothschild thought he needed to also pay them like owners and implemented a profit-sharing plan in 2019 where 20 percent of the firm's annual pre-tax profit is distributed on a pro-rata salary basis among his employees, representing 15 to 20 percent of their total compensation. This profit-sharing is on top of what was already seen as competitive (fair) compensation. Notes Rothschild, "Many were hired long before there was this bonus program."

We asked Rothschild if the employees had any concerns about EBOT – Earnings Before Owner Theft! Owners tend to be aggressive in taking all the write-offs they can, which skews the bottom line.

"There isn't any owner theft," explained Rothschild. "I capped my salary at the start of the plan and my salary will remain at or below the highest-paid employee. My only benefits are gas for my car and health insurance. In fact, my salary at my last venture capital-backed startup was about double my current comp and it came with a major bonus structure too. For me to make serious money, the employees need to get a serious bonus."

"But how might your employees react if you need to invest a significant amount of profit into growth?" we asked. "Moving from stage one to stage two, we don't need to invest profits," Rothschild responded. "Access Fixtures has an optimized cash flow model. All of our manufacturing is contracted out to other lighting manufacturers, and we do not keep any inventory on hand. And Access Fixtures does not require significant capital to support additional sales. We have not needed to touch our operating line of credit for over two years." (This is why the "Cash" section of *Scaling Up (Rockefeller Habits 2.0)* is so important to implement).

So far, Rothschild is very happy with the results: "My people don't work any harder because of the extra check they will receive sometime next year. But they take different decisions, which is good for the company and good for them," he says.

> *"My people don't work any harder because of the extra check they will receive sometime next year. But they take different decisions, which is good for the company and good for them."*

Continues Rothschild: "They can affect anything on the P&L. We are completely open book short of individual salaries. For example, the team knows that a new hire will cost them x dollars plus an eventual share of the 20 percent of the company profits. If they feel we need to spend this to make more money, we will. In other words, while this costs them money, if the new hire increases efficiency and revenue, revenue and profit per employee will increase, netting them a bigger bonus."

"In turn, the employees stopped free lunches once a week. Some even turned down attending a trade show that offered limited corporate value. They gave up being wined and dined," exclaimed Rothschild.

Last, we had to ask Rothschild about his unusual title – he signs his emails as Senior Lighting Specialist. "I am a co-founder, now the only shareholder, as well as the CEO. I use the Senior Lighting Specialist title so that the employees can observe me interacting and selling to customers as an employee just like them. There are very few customers who know that I am CEO and owner," shares Rothschild.

Aligning Interests Through Profit Sharing

Profit-sharing means a company shares a portion of its pre-tax profit with certain groups or all of its employees. Egon Zehnder's formula for distributing profits among its partners, according to seniority, is an example of such a model. Lincoln Electric also has important profit-sharing components in its compensation packages.

In Chapters 3 and 4, we learned that improving *individual* and group performance with financial incentives can be tricky. Yet as discussed, pay schemes like Zehnder's or Access Fixtures' that link rewards to the performance of the entire organization produce far fewer issues. This is because you connect the incentive to important goals of the organization (i.e., pre-tax profit). There are not many goals that compete with *company profit* and therefore it is less likely that such schemes produce goal conflicts, unintended behaviors, or become outdated.

What's the effect of profit-sharing on employee behavior? First and foremost, it is a way of aligning the interests of shareholders and employees (the information effect). Employees tend to decide more like owners when they have skin in the game.

Profit-sharing also helps attract employees and keep them loyal (the selection effect). In some cases, like Lincoln Electric's, the profit pool can become a significant portion of overall compensation. Employees are thus incentivized to stick around until their share is paid out. So, if you payout profits in March or April, after you have closed the books, a new pool has already accumulated, and people think twice before they hop onto the next job (influence godfather Cialdini's discovery that people will do more to avoid a loss than to get a gain!). The same logic applies if you pay out quarterly.

But as Steve Rothschild found out, profit sharing is not effective if you want people to work harder (the motivation effect). A profit goal is too aggregated and detached from people's work, and first-line employees generally have little influence on the outcome. The payout is also too far away from the task.

The problem can be partially overcome with an open-book policy and financial education as promoted by Jack Stack and the Great Game of Business approach. Cascading priorities, KPIs, and a planning process that drives top-down strategy and bottom-up execution, which are at the heart of the Scaling Up methodology, can also provide this critical line-of-sight between the employee's task and the firm's profits.

A Question of Fairness

Apart from producing a desired behavior in people, sharing is also caring – our fifth and last design principle. A profit-sharing scheme is a gesture of fairness and a way for owners to reward those who generated the profit in the first place. Especially when organizations enjoy high profitability, everybody, not only management, should receive a share of the returns that people's hard work has generated.

Brad Hams, in his book *Ownership Thinking*, provides highly practical advice on developing your profit-sharing plan. Please read the details and not just scan the bullet points – there are key insights within each:

- **Eligibility**: It is best to include all employees in the plan, from the cleaning staff to the CEO. It is a way of saying: "We're all in this together, and everybody is focused on profit."

- **Minimum threshold**: Profit-sharing shouldn't happen from the first dollar. Start from a minimum threshold that allows the company to serve a return on capital, be it in the form of a minimum dividend to shareholders, debt repayment, or recapitalization of profits.

- **Profit goal**: The amount of profit that you aspire to generate in the upcoming period should be determined. It is easiest if the goal coincides with your budgeted pre-tax profit. But you can also deviate from that figure and define a stretch (ambitious) goal.

- **Profit share**: Decide the percentage of profits (beyond the minimum threshold) that you want to dedicate to the pool. Brad Hams recommends choosing the share so that the amount awarded to employees corresponds to at least 8-12 percent of the total wage costs when the profit goal is reached. The amount is significant to be appreciated by employees and can justify the administration and communication effort. He would not cap the plan but generously share whatever profit was generated beyond the profit goal.

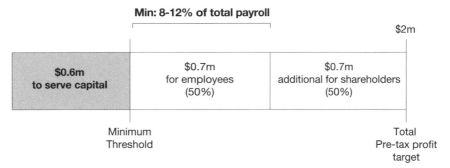

Profit sharing scheme

- **Distribution**: One option is to distribute an equal amount of profit to all employees, independent of their rank. The more common (yet, as we have seen in the case of Heath Ceramics, often not the fairest) solution is to pay the amount in proportion to the employee's base salary. A third option is to differentiate the percentage according to job levels (first-line, coordinators, managers, execs, etc.). TMC adopted this latter approach, paying 8 percent of base salary to entry-level employees, 12 percent to more tenured individual contributors, and 20-25 percent for all leadership positions. This variant reduces the amount of salary at risk for the lower and increases it for the higher ranks. But it also benefits the already better-paid employees disproportionately when things go well and hence contributes further to inequality.

- **Frequency**: Profit sharing is generally done on an annual basis but consider half-yearly or quarterly payouts for lower ranks. To avoid paying money in early quarters and then come in short at the end of the year, you can pay out smaller portions during the first quarters (Q1=10 percent, Q2=20 percent, Q3=30 percent Q4=40 percent). To protect employees against the opposite effect, you can also roll over unearned profit to the following quarter.

- **Conditions**: Consider conditioning the payout based on available cash flow as profitable years can occur with poor cash flow. You also want to pro-rata the payout for people who have recently joined or already left the company.

- **Information sharing**: An open-book policy is critical for any profit-sharing program. Share and explain in emails, on Slack or in town hall meetings your monthly results with all details. "Nothing matters more than those vital statistics – short, frank, frequent reports on how the company is doing," writes management maverick Ricardo Semler, who implemented a generous profit-sharing program at the Brazilian equipment manufacturer Semco. To avoid entitlements, insist that profit shares are "at risk" and that employees should not count on that income. For the same reason, don't give consolation prizes when profits are down.

Bad Profits

The danger of profit-sharing programs is that they can incite short-term thinking, i.e., sacrificing future "good" profits for today's "bad" profits. (Fred Reichheld in *The Ultimate Question* taught us that profits are "bad" if the means of achieving them hurt your long-term profitability, e.g., shortchange customers by delivering a poor experience or pushing overpriced or inappropriate products onto trusting customers). That's why it is best to combine such short-term programs (which are appreciated by employees because they also provide short-term payouts), with long-term, value sharing programs, (e.g., stock, stock options, performance units), which we will discuss now.

Sharing Value with Those Who Create It

After many years in the restaurant industry, Chris Sullivan, co-founder of the restaurant chain Outback Steakhouse realized that the primary challenge for large restaurant chains is maintaining consistency in food quality and service. But why? As he continued to peel back the layers, he concluded that it was due to the industry's average six-month turnover of general managers, a statistic considered to be "just the way it is in the restaurant business."

Good managers were typically moved around to take over for bad managers, and great managers would eventually leave and start their own restaurants. Recognizing manager turnover as the choke point in the industry, Sullivan and his team asked themselves a key question: What if we could keep a restaurant manager in the same restaurant for five to 10 years? This would represent a 10x to 20x improvement over the existing situation in the industry.

The solution to this challenge turned out to be a unique long-term profit/value sharing plan. Sullivan started to ask young talent interested in becoming managers if they would be willing to invest $25,000 in an Outback restaurant. (Imagine your daughter coming home, sharing that she found a job managing a restaurant and that she has to pay $25,000 to get the job.) But here is the deal Sullivan pioneered: New managers would invest $25,000 and commit to staying for five years. Outback would take the first three years to train them to run a restaurant, paying a competitive wage.

During the last two years, the new managers would get to run a restaurant on their own. If they hit certain performance milestones by the fifth year, they would get a $100,000 bonus – a 4x return on their investment – which would vest over the next four years. If they signed on to stay at the same restaurant another five years, they would receive the $100,000 in one lump sum, plus $500,000 worth of stock that would vest over the next five years and expected to double in value (15 percent growth per year). The company ended up turning a bunch of people in their 20s into millionaires.

More importantly, Sullivan's theory was correct. The compensation system actually increased the loyalty of restaurant managers. 90 percent of "proprietors" (the actual title of a manager) stayed in the same restaurant for five years, and 80 percent stayed for ten years or more. This led to higher consistency in food and service quality, which, in turn, delighted customers and helped Outback and its parent company Bloomin' Brands to become one of the largest and best performing restaurant chains in the US with 1,450 outlets and more than $4.1 billion in revenue.

The Effects of Value Sharing

If you would like to share profits with your team but want to avoid the dangers of short-termism, then *value sharing* schemes are an option to consider. Value sharing is the category name for financial instruments that grant employees either real ownership (stock or stock options) or similar economic rights linked to the value of the company (phantom stock, performance units, etc.).

 KEY RESOURCES: *This section on value sharing draws in part from the excellent material created by the compensation consultancy VisionLink and offered on their websites www.vladvisors.com and www.phantomstockonline.com. We recommend that you explore their whitepapers, videos, and assessment tools. Another helpful resource is Steve Poland's Founder's Pocket Guide series on startup funding, for this topic, especially the booklet called Stock Options & Equity Compensation. (If you need to brush up your knowledge around valuation, term sheets, cap tables, equity splits among founders, etc., check out the other volumes as well.)*

How are value-sharing schemes different from short-term incentives? Do they have the same effects on employee behavior? Yes and no.

Value sharing has a strong selection *effect*. People are attracted to value-sharing programs by the perspective of building additional wealth on top of their salary. In markets with talent shortages like Silicon Valley, companies of all sizes are practically forced to send this signal. Top-notch engineers or successful digital marketers wouldn't even consider an offer if the package doesn't contain a piece of equity. Once people are on board, value-sharing programs also have a retention effect because of the long payout and vesting periods of these instruments. Outback Steakhouse is a case in point.

Value-sharing programs also communicate what is important to employees (*information effect*). Partial ownership is enough to reinforce the role of employees as stewards of the company's assets and interests. Owners and employees share the risks and rewards associated with the business activity and align their interests through these programs. Employees who are also owners think and act more long-term, strategically, and holistically.

But just like profit sharing, value-sharing programs don't have a *motivational effect*. People might make different decisions and set other priorities, but they generally won't dispense discretionary effort because they have shares in your company.

Share with the Entire Team

Nevertheless, the selection and information effects alone have a positive impact on a company's value and justify the implementation of these programs. Research by Richard Freeman from Harvard University shows that broad-based employee ownership, especially when combined with policies that empower employees and create a positive workplace culture, increases the return on equity and makes companies more valuable.

As with profit-sharing, it is beneficial to allow all employees to participate in the growing value of a company. Freeman's research shows that the broad-based programs are the most successful.

This was also Google's policy since its early days. In the beginning, stock and stock options were the only currency the young company had to attract top talent. Up until the IPO in 2004, almost every new hire took a cut in salary that had to be compensated with upside potential in the company's stock. By the way, that included Bonnie Brown, a masseuse at Google when they were 40 employees. Brown was paid $450 a week plus a pile of options she thought would never be worth anything. Today, Brown is a multimillionaire who gets a daily massage herself and does charitable work through her own foundations. With now over 135,000 people, everybody at Google still receives stock awards based on individual performance. "We don't have to include everyone, but it is good business and the right thing to do," writes Laszlo Bock, former VP of People Operations at Google, in his book *Work Rules!*

We agree. First, sharing the generated value with everyone is a sign of appreciation and respect toward those who helped create it. Second, value-sharing programs and growth are mutually reinforcing. As Freeman's research shows, value-sharing programs increase a company's value, which in turn creates the currency needed to fuel these programs.

But it's not only Silicon Valley that understands the value of making employees owners. Industrial firms like Chobani and Harley Davidson have granted large amounts of stock to their team, including all their blue-collar workers. Chobani, which in 2016 granted 10 percent of its shares to employees, has recently filed for an IPO - a move that will make many of its first-line workers millionaires. "This isn't a gift," said Chobani's founder and CEO Hamdi Ulukaya to his team when announcing the plan. "It's a mutual promise to work together with a shared purpose and responsibility. To continue to create something special and of lasting value."

Interestingly, even profit-hungry private equity firms like KKR & Co. have started to see the power of employee ownership programs. KKR now grants options to 100 percent of staff in the industrial companies they acquire - with impressive results in terms of engagement, financial performance, and wealth creation for blue-collar workers. Search for the video "2018 KKR Investor Day - Pete Stavros" to get details of this impactful story (tears included). In fact, it was KKR Partner Pete Stavros who inspired Harley Davidson's CEO, Jochen Zeitz, to make a similar move and grant stock to all of its 4,500 workers in the middle of the Covid crisis in February 2021.

How much value should you share? This depends on how much your owners are willing to give up and how much upside you will create. Companies that don't grow don't have value to share.

Options for Value-Sharing

There are several ways of implementing a value-sharing program. The particular form these take depends on the regulation of each country. VisionLink developed a useful overview of the nine main instruments available under US legislation in the form of a decision tree. You find the decision tree, detailed descriptions of each of these instruments, plus advice on how to implement them on their website *www.phantomstockonline.com*. We reproduce the decision tree in a simpler form below.

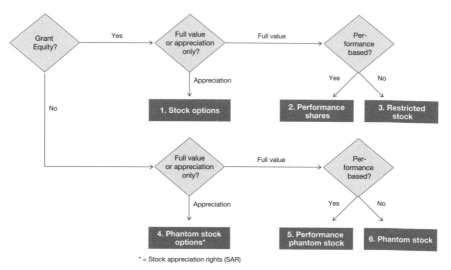

Value sharing options

The illustration above shows that there are two main decisions that owners need to make when designing a value sharing scheme:

1. Do I want to grant equity with full ownership rights (options 1-3) or only surrogates that allow the employee to participate in the value creation but not obtain the decisions and information rights of a shareholder (options 4-6)?

2. Do I allow employees to participate in the full value of the company (2,3,5,6) or only in the appreciation of the value from the moment you grant these titles (1,4)?

A third decision you need to make (not reflected in the illustration) is whether to *grant* (i.e., a gift) the stock or *sell* it to the employee. This has obvious consequences on cash flow for both sides but also on taxes. Grants are taxable income for the employee, although the tax would be deferred if the stock is restricted with a vesting clause. The grant would also be a deductible expense for the company.

Deciding on the right tool or combination thereof requires a solid analysis of your situation, including the legal options in the countries you operate in and the tax consequences for both employer and employee. This makes it impossible for us to recommend a specific tool. However, we *do* want to make a case for three options that, in our experience, are too rarely considered among scaleups. These are a public offering, employee stock ownership plans (ESOP), and phantom stock.

Mid-Market Firms Going Public

Before you dismiss reading this section, see the IKE example below (went public at $3 million in revenue). We know few mid-market companies consider an IPO. They are afraid of losing control, public scrutiny, and high administrative costs. Yet, when it comes to pay, an IPO can become a game-changer because it equips you with a currency (stock and options) your competitor might not have. And contrary to popular belief, you don't need to be big or profitable to go public.

Creating this additional currency to reward great talent is an important reason why Microsoft went public early on. It didn't need the cash. Instead, it was an effective way to have the "public" give their people significant compensation. If you're a private firm, an extra dollar in profit means you only have that dollar to share. In a public company, every dollar you take to the bottom line generates 15 – 100x in liquidity you can share with employees, depending on your price to earnings (PE) ratio.

You could argue that you do not need to go public to grant your employees stock. Yet, the big difference is liquidity. Your employees can sell their publicly-traded stock at any time to make a down payment on a house or pay for a medical emergency. If the company is private, they might not find anyone willing to buy their stock, at least not at the valuation that they consider attractive. And the liquidity of the stock by itself makes a huge difference in the valuation of the firm. Investors might pay twice the price for a share that they can sell whenever they want.

The Colorado based firm IKE, a long standing Scaling Up practitioner, took this path and went public extremely early in its life. IKE provides monitoring services and data analysis for millions of infrastructure poles as electricity and telecom providers own them across the country (AT&T and Verizon are clients). The firm was founded in 2012 and went public in 2014 on the New Zealand and the Australian stock exchanges simultaneously. At that point, it only had 21 employees, less than $3 million in revenue, and losses bigger than revenue.

Paying high fixed salaries to attract talent or investing in R&D while making big losses is difficult. In these cases, an IPO can be an excellent strategy to afford these things and accelerate growth. It worked in the case of IKE. A subscription-based business model, strong patents, and attractive growth perspectives in the US were sufficiently attractive to raise $18 million at a valuation of $39 million during the IPO.

Today, the company is valued at $84 million. The employees don't have the most competitive salaries in the industry, but most of them own stock or options and with that have a solid incentive to continue the ride.

Rich or King

The wealth created for your team in an IPO can become a critical differentiator in your overall strategy.

SAS Institute and Microsoft, two software companies that were born at the same time, provide an interesting case study of the impact that choices around value sharing can have on the trajectory of a firm.

SAS Institute, the North Carolina-based data analytics software house we introduced in Chapter 3, was founded as a spin-off from NC State University by four partners in 1976. The company was profitable from the first year (and ever since), never took venture capital, and is still owned today by two of the original founders, James Goodnight and John Sall. Employees are compensated with a fixed salary at about market average. SAS has never offered sign-up bonuses, performance bonuses, stock options, phantom shares, or the like (it does have a small profit-sharing scheme). In 2020, SAS had 14,000 employees and a revenue of $3.1 billion. James Goodnight owns 67 percent of SAS, John Sall 33 percent.

Microsoft, which was founded just one year earlier, chose a different route. It took on venture capital in 1981, went public in 1985, and its bonuses and stock awards have so far created four billionaires and more than 12,000 millionaires (almost equal to SAS's total number of employees). Microsoft had 163,000 employees and $143 billion in revenue in 2020. Bill Gates currently owns one percent of Microsoft and is the second richest person in the world, according to *Forbes*.

No doubt, SAS is an extraordinary success story, and Goodnight and Sall would probably not want to have it any other way. But the founders' preference for remaining private and not creating the attractive currency of stock options put SAS onto a very different trajectory and undoubtedly contributed to the fact that SAS is today only a fraction of Microsoft in revenues, employees, and valuation.

Another case in point for the impact of going public on compensation is Southwest Airlines, the world's most successful airline of all times. Disposing of the currency of publicly-traded stock proved to be a critical component of its strategy. It gave the late Herb Kelleher, their iconic CEO, a key negotiating tool with the unions. He traded important wage concessions, in support of Southwest's low-cost strategy, for stock. Chris Sullivan, co-founder of Outback Steakhouse, did the same when he used the public's money to retain his restaurant "proprietors."

As the illustration on page 20 in Chapter 1 also suggests, your owners' expectations regarding growth, profitability, and return on capital are important design parameters for your compensation system. Are your shareholders ambitious venture capitalists who want to multiply their investment several times over during the coming years? Or are you running a family business, where the main concern is security and sustainability for the next generations? What is the long-term financial plan that needs to be supported by the compensation system?

For entrepreneurs, such questions often crystallize in the choice between "King" or "Rich," which Noam Wasserman describes in his book *The Founder's Dilemma*. It's a classic quandary for entrepreneurs. Do you want to be "King" which stands for retaining control of the company you founded, in exchange for slower growth and less wealth? Or do you want to be "Rich" which represents equity dilution and loss of control for the founders, in benefit of faster growth and a higher payout.

Wasserman's research found that staying "King" does not pay off financially: Statistically, the smaller slice of a bigger pie is twice as valuable as the bigger slice of the smaller pie, as the parallel stories of Microsoft and SAS Institute illustrate.

Drawbacks to Equity Sharing

The decision of business owners to share the value created with their teams is right and laudable. We have mentioned several good reasons for doing that. But sharing equity also has some drawbacks from the owner's and the employee's perspective.

Granting stock to your employees is entering a business partnership with them. Business partnerships are complex and end up in divorce more often than marriages. One might still be the majority owner but granting formal ownership rights to employees can create some nuisances as well. It is easy to end up fighting over strategy, investments, dividends, or salaries. And, in the case of private companies, the question is what happens when the employee leaves, or you want her to leave. Do you let her keep the stock? Do you buy it back? At what valuation? Do you have the cash to buy it back at that moment?

Dan Price learned this lesson the hard way when his older brother and co-founder of Gravity Payments, Lucas Price, sued him to be bought out of the company. Lucas wasn't on board with the $70k minimum salary decision; accused Dan of "socialist business practices;" and feared that he was ruining the company they had built together. In 2015, Lucas filed suit for breach of contract, breach of fiduciary duty, and minority shareholder oppression, attempting a forced sale of his minority stake for $26 million. In July 2016, a judge ruled in favor of Dan Price on all counts. The story shows that sometimes even brotherly love is not a strong enough bond to keep business partners aligned when millions are at stake.

There are drawbacks for the employees as well: First, an employee needs to purchase the stock with cash, or pay income tax on the full value, in case it is granted by the company. Employees often don't have the means or willingness to do that. The other inconvenience is the already mentioned illiquidity of stock in private companies. There is no market for small minority stakes in private companies. If existing shareholders are willing to buy at all, they might use the lack of a market to their advantage and ask for a steep discount.

Employee Stock Ownership Plans

An Employee Stock Ownership Plan (ESOP) is a form of equity sharing with significant tax advantages for owners and employees that is unique to the US. More than 14 million US workers in 6,500 companies are part of such a plan, according to the National Center of Employee Ownership. Palmer-Donavin, a distributor of building materials in Columbus, Ohio, with 560 employees and $280 million in revenue, started such a plan in 2007. The company was precisely 100 years old when the three majority owner families wanted to sell the business because none of them had any heirs actively involved in the business.

After considering private equity and strategic buyers, the owners decided to sell all their shares to an ESOP trust that the company set up for its employees.

They saw in the ESOP a tool to engage and retain employees and also a formula to sell the business while preserving their legacy. In this particular case, the decision to sell was influenced by the fact that the sale had significant tax advantages for the owners if the employees would buy all the shares through the ESOP trust (concrete tax advantages depend, among other things, on the legal form of your company).

At inception, the trust had no assets and took on a loan from the company and subordinated debt from the three majority owners. With these loans, the trust then purchased the shares from the owners at fair market value (a so-called leveraged ESOP). The loan from the owners was paid back after only three years. The internal company loan will be fully paid off in 2026, 20 years after the plan was put in place.

After this initial transfer of ownership, Palmer-Donavin became exempt from corporate income tax because the shares were now held by a qualified retirement plan. In practice, that means that 100 percent of profits go to the ESOP every year. While other formulas are possible, Palmer-Donavin allocates these profits based on the employee's proportion of total company salaries. "If my payroll equals half a percent of the overall company's payroll, I get half a percentage of shares allocated for that year," explains Shawn Richard, vice president of HR.

What makes ESOPs so attractive from the employees' perspective is that they don't have to pay income tax on the contribution they receive in stock until they take a distribution, usually when they resign or retire from the firm, and the ESOP trust repurchases their shares. Palmer-Donavin grants shares to new employees after six months of service, but the shares vest over six years. This serves as an excellent retention mechanism for talented employees who don't want to lose the equity they have accumulated. And such patience is in order. The next frontline employee who will retire under the tenure of the current CEO, Robyn Pollina, will leave as a millionaire. This has been a stated company goal for years.

A myriad of studies has shown that employee ownership generally leads to better performance. That's also the case for ESOPs. "Statistically, companies with ESOPs and Ownership Thinking cultures significantly outperform not only their previous years' performance but also the performances of their non-ESOP competitors," writes Brad Hams in his book *Ownership Thinking*. But these plans need to be implemented with a lot of thought and attention to detail, especially in terms of communication. Companies that don't educate their people, communicate well, and create the appropriate ownership culture actually underperform, writes Hams.

This is also the experience at Palmer-Donavin. "It doesn't automatically make people care about the company," remarks Robyn Pollina. "If you don't have an employee-first culture, it's probably not going to resonate." But Palmer-Donavin embraced servant leadership long before the ESOP, Pollina says. "And now we treat our employees like shareholders because they are." To remind employees of the value of the plan, the company produces a benefits statement each year that shows them what went into their ESOP.

Palmer-Donavin has found that an ESOP is costly to maintain, given compliance and administrative burdens. "Yet, the biggest cost associated with the ESOP is that you are essentially recapitalizing yourself constantly," explains Shawn Richard. "You have to have really good cash flow to make the ESOP possible. You're constantly buying out shares. If you have 560 employees and 100 leave, we have to have the cash to buy those shares out."

Beyond the ESOP, employees at Palmer-Donavin are also eligible for a 401(k) retirement plan, where the company provides a matching contribution. Employees are automatically enrolled, and there is an automatic step-up. "We want them to be prudent investors," says Richard. "If, God forbid, the company was going to suffer a financial calamity, they won't end up with their money in a single stock."

Palmer Donavin's benefits package has definitely given the company an edge during the post-covid labor shortage, according to Richard. "Over the last year, we added 90 employees to our payroll," he says. "At the same time, we reduced our turnover rate. We have the lowest turnover rate in seven years."

For Palmer-Donavin, the ESOP represented an additional advantage when it comes to the firm's growth strategy. After the plan was implemented, the firm made two significant acquisitions adding almost 260 employees to the team. "When we acquired these companies, the owners were selling all shares to an ESOP, which for them was tax-exempt," explains CEO Robyn Pollina. "With similar offers on the table, a selling owner is much better off from a tax perspective selling to an ESOP versus a non-ESOP."

As we have seen in the case of Palmer Donavin, ESOPs have many advantages but also their share of challenges. You should definitely stay away from them if you are not profitable (you won't be able to repurchase shares from employees who leave) or too small to bear the overhead cost (< 25 people approx.). Lack of profitability and cash is also why startups with an exit on the horizon are better off with option plans than ESOPs. They need all their cash for growth and can't afford to repurchase shares from employees who leave the boat.

In any case, get solid legal and financial advice before you pursue an ESOP. If you want unbiased and well-researched information, we suggest you check out the books, papers, and other resources the National Center for Employee Ownership offers at *www.nceo.org*.

Phantom Stock

Last, let´s look at phantom stock as an alternative to an equity program that avoids the many issues around governance and control (yet it doesn't solve the liquidity challenge). Phantom stock is a private contract between company and employee wherein the company promises to pay cash to the employee upon certain conditions. The agreement replicates the financial outcomes of granting restricted stock but with fewer strings attached. An example works best to illustrate the mechanic:

Let's assume your company is valued at $15 million, and you issue 1.5 million phantom shares. Each share is worth $10. You decide to grant your long-serving CFO Rajeev 20,000 shares. The phantom shares have a value of $200,000 at the time they are awarded. At that moment, they have no cash or tax consequences, neither for you nor for Rajeev. Let's assume further that after the vesting period of four years, the value of the company has increased fourfold to $60 million. Company value divided by the number of phantom shares gives a share price of $40; hence Rajeev's shares are now worth $800,000. When you pay Rajeev this amount, he must pay income tax (instead of capital gains tax in the case of equity), but with the advantage that the tax is only due when he actually receives cash, not when the shares are granted, as is the case with equity.

What's compelling about this solution is that Rajeev receives a significant reward, with similar upside potential as equity but without the potential headaches that come with shared ownership. Phantom stock will not be the right choice for everyone (e.g., stock options are much better if you are going for an IPO), but we would encourage you to explore this less-known option. For more details on phantom stock and how they compare to equity, read the insightful and practical whitepaper, *Phantom Stock - The Ideal Plan for Growing Private Companies*, which you find on *www.vladvisors.com*.

Closing:
Get Pay Right and
Out of Sight

We shared from the beginning, the way you compensate people is one of the most important strategic decisions you will make. Scaling a company is difficult enough. To overcome the unfavorable odds, you need all the energy you can get from your people. A fair and clever compensation plan is indispensable for this.

The plan needs to be fair in the sense that employees feel their salary is an expression of your respect, appreciation, and equitable treatment. Take special care of those at the lower end of the pyramid and pay them generous *living*, not *minimum* wages. That's often the starting point of a Good Jobs Strategy that can ripple through your entire ecosystem and benefit all stakeholders.

A clever system means two things. First, your compensation plans consider the inscrutable nature of human psychology – the counterintuitive and irrational perceptions and reactions people have to compensation decisions.

Second, you must deploy pay systems that serve your strategy and reinforce your culture. We have seen the limitations of financial incentives, but you have also read about formidable examples of companies that ingeniously use comp schemes to influence decisions and behaviors of employees in the interests of customers and other stakeholders.

In a perfect world, you wouldn't need comp plans to make your people behave in a certain way. In an ideal world, movers would be intrinsically motivated not to break stuff. Hildebrand's team would be naturally driven to double the oil and gas reserves. Zehnder's headhunters would receive fat bonuses without adopting a "selling" attitude and go for the quick money.

But our world is not perfect. We need to acknowledge this reality and use pay systems, in ethical ways, to nudge people into doing the right thing for the different stakeholders of our firms. Not using these tools represents a considerable opportunity cost and makes scaling your business more difficult.

This pragmatic approach worked for TMC as well. Compensation was only one of several People practices that Sebastian and his team used to execute on TMC's strategy and reinforce its culture. TMC's growth story was, to a substantial degree, the result of its "strange" People practices. And the story ended well.

In November 2017, the Swiss-based Unilabs, Europe's second-largest diagnostic group, acquired the company at an unusually high multiple for industry standards. Intangibles like strategy, medical and technical talent, software, processes, and the general "strangeness" of the firm's culture helped justify a high acquisition price in the eyes of the new owners.

We hope this book guides you in making these critical (and expensive) compensation decisions. But also remember that pay is not the only tool in your toolbox. Thoughtful selection, job enrichment with challenging tasks and projects, coaching people, good communication, recognition, making work meaningful – all these practices foster behaviors and create culture in more sustainable ways than financial incentives ever could.

So again, get pay right and out of sight. The way people are treated at work has a far bigger influence on performance than the money you pay them. Fail to provide these other "total rewards" and you'll have to pay people a whole lot more!

Appendix

Appendix A: Six Principles of Persuasion

In his bestselling book *Influence: The Psychology of Persuasion*, behavioral psychologist and Dr. Robert Cialdini explains the psychology of why people say yes and how to apply these principles ethically in business and everyday situations. Here come the six principles, applied by us to the context of compensation:

1) **Reciprocity** – This is the very essence of compensation, trading value for value. You do something for me, and I feel obligated to return the favor. It is this principle that drives whether compensation is perceived to be fair or not.

2) **Scarcity** – Know why some jobs are worth more than others and be able to articulate it.

3) **Authority** – Recognize how compensation studies, such as the Hay Executive Compensation Report, tend to inflate compensation rates, especially across executive ranks. In turn, showing how your own pay rates compare favorably in your market can take pressure off the compensation conversation.

4) **Commitment and consistency** – This underpins why a gazillion frequent and small rewards are more effective in shaping behavior than a few big rewards.

5) **Liking** – If an employee likes working for the company, it reduces the pressure on the monetary side of compensation. And if the employee is liked, that often positively influences their comp, as well.

6) **Consensus** – There is a lot of pressure to conform to the norms of other compensation systems, so you must over-communicate the reasons your compensation approach is different.

As Dr. Cialdini warns, what has the power to do good has the power to do evil. So, we share these principles simply to get you thinking about the psychological aspects of compensation. And they work both ways. Employees can employ these principles in seeking greater compensation, as much as employers can can use them to inform their decisions. Again, compensation decisions are as much psychological as they are logical. Study up on human psychology and behavior by reading both of Dr. Cialdini's books *Influence* and *Pre-Suasion*.

Appendix B: Total Rewards Statement

A total reward statement is intended to provide an employee with an overview of the monetary value of her total rewards. It puts a dollar value on items like bonus, stock rights, vacation, health insurance, car, gym, cafeteria, vacation, sick days, etc. It makes potential trade-offs between such concepts visible and facilitates comparisons with other firms.

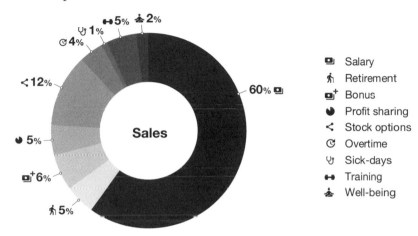

Below is a graphical representation of the benefits that Nike used to offer its employees.

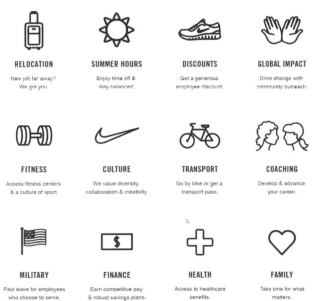

Appendix C: Compensation Philosophy Statement

If you consider writing your own compensation philosophy statement, here are few more references that can help create your own.

- Ken Gibson from the VisionLink, a compensation consultancy, explains why it is important to define your compensation philosophy and how to go about it: *https://blog.vladvisors.com/blog/why-a-pay-philosophy-is-a-ceos-best-friend*

- The extremely transparent social media company Buffer shares on its blog many articles on its compensation philosophy and also real salary data. This is their latest update: *https://buffer.com/resources/compensation-philosophy/*

- This thoughtful overview on compensation in startups written by the venture fund Homebrew is also a good reference when defining your compensation philosophy and other practical elements of your compensation system: *https://quip.com/HEB3Ah9dYD6o*

- KPMG offers advice and further reference on how to create your own pay philosophy - *https://home.kpmg/content/dam/kpmg/ng/pdf/tax/ng-compensation-philosophy.pdf*

Below you also find an example of a compensation philosophy statement for a fictitious company we created. It suggests a structure that can be a starting point for your own work.

COMPENSATION PHILOSOPHY

What is the role of compensation in our organization?
This item speaks to the importance of pay in your culture. What weight do you give financial and non-financial rewards? To what degree do you expect pay to drive behavior and results?

- *We offer highly attractive compensation packages and excellent working conditions to attract the very best talent. And because we only hire the very best, we expect our people to be at least twice as productive as the average worker in our industry (revenue/team member).*

- *We consider pay to be a hygiene factor. We want to get pay right and out of sight. We don't want people to think about money. We want them to focus on our core purpose and be intrinsically motivated to do great work - because they are professionals and enjoy what they do, not because we pay them.*

- *We don't expect people to work harder because we pay them more money. But we hope that our financial incentives make people take decisions and set priorities that benefit all stakeholders in the long term and in an equitable way. Creating shareholder value is an important objective but not the only one. It needs to be balanced with the long-term interests of other stakeholders.*

How should the created value be shared?
This asks you to define the expectation of shareholders regarding their return on capital and how remaining profit and value should be shared among stakeholders.

- *Our shareholders expect an annual return on their capital of 12 percent. This portion of profits is mainly reinvested but can also be paid out as dividends.*

- *The pre-tax profits that exceed the 12 percent hurdle shall be shared in the form of a profit-sharing plan between shareholders and employees.*

- *Increases in the company value are shared via a long-term, value-sharing program with senior executives and selected key contributors.*

What is our pay positioning relative to the market?
This item addresses what the organization wants to pay relative to the market for base salary and total compensation.

- *We establish base salaries at the 75th percentile of the market. For total compensation, we aspire to be at the 95th percentile. Together with our brand, our culture, and our benefits, our total rewards package should position us as a top three employer in our industry worldwide.*

What pay components do we offer, and what is the proportion between them?
Address the way base pay is structured and speak to the different elements of variable compensation and their proportion to guaranteed components. Explain how employees can increase their pay.

- *Base salary is determined by a pay structure with pay grades. The spread between the minimum and maximum of each grade is wide, and grades have significant overlap between them. This allows us to reward outstanding performance within the same pay grade. It can also lead to situations where a team member has a higher salary than his/her manager.*

- *In addition to a base salary, we offer a short-term profit-sharing program. Profits are distributed in proportion to people's base salary. Colleagues with lower salary are assigned absolute amounts.*

- *The value-sharing program awards a percentage of base salary in the form of stock, stock options or similar instruments annually.*

- *For the vast majority of our team members, the base salary represents 85 percent or more of total compensation. Salespeople and managers should receive at least 35 percent of their total compensation as variable components.*

- *We don't offer individual and group incentive schemes. They regularly produce effects that are not in the overall interest of the company. Behavior should be guided by our culture, our planning system, as well as frequent coaching, not by financial incentives.*

- *Variable pay is contingent on results. Without results, there will be no variable pay. Clear communication must avoid entitlements.*

- *Team members can increase their compensation through annual merit raises and promotions to higher pay grades, both based on individual and team performance. Further opportunities to increase compensation exist through the annual profits sharing and the long-term value-sharing program, which are both uncapped.*

Who decides on pay?

Who decides what and when around compensation? How do you deal with compensation in the budgeting process?

- *Our CEO is ultimately accountable for everything concerned with talent and compensation. Decisions about the compensation system are generally taken by the senior leadership team. Decisions regarding the compensation of individuals within the given system are made by a compensation committee, based on the suggestion of the direct supervisor. Salaries are adjusted once a year as part of the budgeting process. The CEO leads the compensation committee.*

Appendix D: Market References

Your compensation system needs to be tailored to your context (culture, strategy, non-financial rewards, etc.), but it is also important to be aware of how your packages compare to others in the market.

For the US, Salary.com offers a subscription to its salary database, filtered for your geography and industry, and with hundreds of job titles to choose from. Subscription prices start at around $1,000 per year for one location. One-time reports for single positions are more affordable and some simple features are even free. PayScale is an alternative provider for the US and some other locations (e.g., Canada and the UK). For other regions, you would have to research local providers. LinkedIn offers a global free salary reference tool, but coverage is still limited. Glassdoor also provides international information on salaries.

Advanced HR offers aggregated compensation data from 1,700 venture-backed companies, including detailed information on bonuses and equity packages. The data is excellent as the who's who of the venture capital industry (Kleiner Perkins, Andreessen Horowitz, Accel, Techstars, etc.) offer the tool to their portfolio companies who, in return, feed their salaries into the database. Traditional compensation consultants like Towers Perrin, Hewitt Associates, or Mercer offer international coverage but at a steep price point.

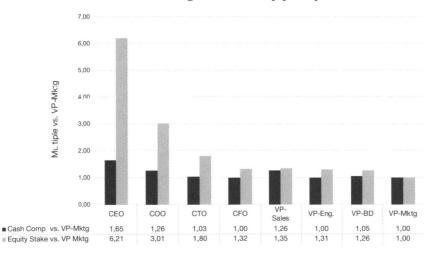

	CEO	COO	CTO	CFO	VP-Sales	VP-Eng.	VP-BD	VP-Mktg
■ Cash Comp vs. VP-Mktg	1,65	1,26	1,03	1,00	1,26	1,00	1,05	1,00
▧ Equity Stake vs. VP Mktg	6,21	3,01	1,80	1,32	1,35	1,31	1,26	1,00

Non-founder Executive relative compensation

References for fixed salary and equity compensation of leadership teams can be found in Noam Wasserman's research. Wasserman, an entrepreneurship professor at USC and author of *The Founder's Dilemma*, offers real-life references of compensation levels for non-founder, C-level hires in technology and life science startups. In his dataset (3,600 US startups, 6.8 years old, average 28 FTE, 10 years of data), non-founding CEOs averaged equity stakes of 6 percent, COOs 2.9 percent, CTOs 1.7 percent, and CFOs 1.3 percent. Interesting also is the relative cash and equity compensation of the different C-Suite functions in relation to the VP-Marketing as depicted in the chart above. (Even more interesting is that the *Chief People Officer* doesn't even appear on this list – a big miss in our view!)

Venture capitalist and blogger Fred Wilson (Twitter, Tumblr, Zynga, Kickstarter) had the right idea in a blog post entitled, "Employee Equity: How Much?" He offered a formula to calculate the percentage of equity you should give to each hierarchy level. The compensation that comes out of this formula seems somewhat low and dated (unless you are growing very rapidly) but the formula, as such, is a great way to structure the problem. Equity percentages are not the best reference point, anyhow. Especially if you are running a fast-growing business with a quickly increasing company valuation, you should be thinking more about absolute dollar terms and not percentages.

 TIP: *If you are struggling with a fair equity distribution among founders, then read Noam Wasserman's book* The Founder's Dilemmas *(chapters 6 and 8) for help. For tips on structuring term sheets in an equity round to protect founders as well as employee-owners, read* Venture Deals *by Brad Feld and Jason Mendelson and the above-mentioned* Founder's Pocket Guide *series by Steve Poland. The National Center for Employee Ownership (www.nceo.org) offers a wealth of information as well.*

About the Authors

Verne Harnish is founder of the world-renowned Entrepreneurs' Organization (EO), with over 15,000 members worldwide, and chaired for fifteen years EO's premiere CEO program, the "Birthing of Giants" held at MIT, a program in which he still teaches today.

Founder and CEO of Scaling Up, a global executive education and coaching company with over 190 partners on six continents, Verne has spent the past three decades helping companies scaleup.

He's the author of the bestseller *Mastering the Rockefeller Habits*; and along with the editors of *Fortune*, authored *The Greatest Business Decisions of All Times*, for which Jim Collins wrote the foreword. His third book *Scaling Up (Rockefeller Habits 2.0)* has been translated into 19 languages and has won eight major international book awards including the prestigious International Book Award for Best General Business book.

Verne also chairs the annual ScaleUp Summits and serves on several boards including vice chair of The Riordan Clinic; co-founder and chair of Geoversity; and board member of the social venture Million Dollar Women. A private investor in many scaleups, Verne enjoys piano, tennis, and magic as a card-carrying member of the International Brotherhood of Magicians.

***

Sebastian Ross is a thought leader and consultant in the space of People, Culture, and Conscious Business. Sebastian started his career as an entrepreneur in the technology space and later as a partner in a venture capital firm. In recent years, Sebastian held leadership roles as CEO and other C-level positions with several international scaleups. Sebastian lectures occasionally on People practices for scaleups and Conscious Capitalism at different Spanish Universities. He is currently the Director of the School of Founders-Program for scaleup entrepreneurs at the IESE Business School in Barcelona.

Sebastian co-founded the Spanish chapter of Entrepreneurs' Organization (EO) and was a board member for many years. He co-founded the Spanish Conscious Capitalism chapter and is currently the President of the Spanish Conscious Capitalism Foundation.

Sebastian received a Ph.D. and an MBA from the University of Cologne, a Master of International Business Administration from ESADE Business

School in Barcelona. He participated in the Entrepreneurial Masters Program at the Massachusetts Institute of Technology. He is also an elected member of the Royal European Academy of Doctors.

Sebastian is German and has been living in Barcelona for over 20 years. He is married and has two sons.